Social Safety and Security

Social Safety and Security

Special Issue Editor
Joannes Chliaoutakis

MDPI • Basel • Beijing • Wuhan • Barcelona • Belgrade

Special Issue Editor
Joannes Chliaoutakis
Hellenic Mediterranean University
Greece

Editorial Office
MDPI
St. Alban-Anlage 66
4052 Basel, Switzerland

This is a reprint of articles from the Special Issue published online in the open access journal *Safety* (ISSN 2313-576X) in 2019 (available at: https://www.mdpi.com/journal/safety/special_issues/Social_Safety_and_Security).

For citation purposes, cite each article independently as indicated on the article page online and as indicated below:

LastName, A.A.; LastName, B.B.; LastName, C.C. Article Title. *Journal Name* **Year**, *Article Number*, Page Range.

ISBN 978-3-03928-146-6 (Pbk)
ISBN 978-3-03928-147-3 (PDF)

© 2020 by the authors. Articles in this book are Open Access and distributed under the Creative Commons Attribution (CC BY) license, which allows users to download, copy and build upon published articles, as long as the author and publisher are properly credited, which ensures maximum dissemination and a wider impact of our publications.

The book as a whole is distributed by MDPI under the terms and conditions of the Creative Commons license CC BY-NC-ND.

Contents

About the Special Issue Editor vii

Preface to "Social Safety and Security" ix

Sanni Yaya and Bishwajit Ghose
Alcohol Drinking by Husbands/Partners Is Associated with Higher Intimate Partner Violence against Women in Angola
Reprinted from: *Safety* **2019**, *5*, 5, doi:10.3390/safety5010005 1

Maria Papadakaki, Angelos Tsalkanis, Dimitra Prokopiadou, Martha Goutsou and Joannes Chliaoutakis
Is Sexual Assault a Problem in Greek Prisons? Initial Evidence from a Greek Male Prison
Reprinted from: *Safety* **2019**, *5*, 84, doi:10.3390/safety5040084 13

Julia C. Babcock and Jason Cooper
Testing the Utility of the Neural Network Model to Predict History of Arrest among Intimate Partner Violent Men
Reprinted from: *Safety* **2019**, *5*, 2, doi:10.3390/safety5010002 29

Melody M. Terras, Gillian Hendry and Dominic Jarret
The Challenges of Safety and Community Integration for Vulnerable Individuals
Reprinted from: *Safety* **2019**, *5*, 85, doi:10.3390/safety5040085 40

Tor-Olav Nævestad, Alexandra Laiou, Ross O. Phillips, Torkel Bjørnskau and George Yannis
Safety Culture among Private and Professional Drivers in Norway and Greece: Examining the Influence of National Road Safety Culture
Reprinted from: *Safety* **2019**, *5*, 20, doi:10.3390/safety5020020 58

Vagioula Tsoutsi, Dimitris Dikeos, Maria Basta and Maria Papadakaki
Driving Behaviour in Depression: Findings from a Driving Simulator Study
Reprinted from: *Safety* **2019**, *5*, 70, doi:10.3390/safety5040070 91

About the Special Issue Editor

Joannes Chliaoutakis (MSc, PhD). He is an Emeritus Professor of sociology at the Department of Social Work of the Hellenic Mediterranean University (HMU) and researcher in the Laboratory of Health and Road Safety. He served as the Head of the Department of Social Work from 2004 till 2006. Since 2009, he has been the Head of the School of Health and Social Welfare Sciences, HMU in Crete. Since 2005, he has been a member of the Executive Board of the Master's Degree Program "Environmental & Occupational Health-Management & Financial Assessment" organized by the Medical School, University of Athens. Since 1988, he has worked as a researcher in the Greek Institute of Child Health, the -EC project, and the European Longitudinal Study of Pregnancy & Childhood. He has published several papers in international and national scientific journals in the field of road safety, sexual and reproductive health, HIV/AIDS and Assisted Reproductive Technologies. He served as the Director of Studies for the project "Gender & Equity" of the Operational Programme for Education and Initial Vocational Training (O.P. "Education") from 2005 till 2009. Recently, he has been involved in various EC projects concerning safe driving behaviour, e.g. the COST action 357 Accident Prevention Options with Motorcycle Helmets; the COST action TU1101 Helmet Optimization in Europe; the three-year project titled "Reducing the harm and the burden of injuries and human loss caused by road traffic crashes and addressing injury demands through effective interventions" (as a Coordinator) carried out in Greece, Germany and Italy with funding by the DG Mobility and Transport (MOVE/C4/SUB/2011-294/SI2.628846/REHABIL-AID); the MOBIHAVE project (*the use of mobile phones while driving*, supported by national funds). In addition, he has worked on projects dealing with gender role and differences, e.g. the *Youth Sexual Violence* 2009 1222 (EAHC); and, two DAPHNE projects (JUST/2011-2012/DAP/AG/3272 and JUST/2011-2012/DAP/AG/3008) on *sexual harassment and violence against women* (in the one as a Coordinator). Finally, he has over 50 research articles (since 2014, he has received over 850 citations and gained an h-index of 18).

Preface to "Social Safety and Security"

As most experienced readers appreciate the international scientific review of Safety for its unique perspective on vulnerable individuals and risk-related behaviours in various manifestations of our daily life, we have organized the publication of a Special Issue that focuses on a number of contemporary issues in social safety and security. This publication provides the latest research in important thematic areas, highlighting intimate partner violence against women, alcohol use, inmate sexual victimization of males during incarceration, and the utility of modern models to predict the history of arrest among intimate partner violent men. Similarly, findings are presented for vulnerable individuals concerning the challenges of their safety and community integration. Within the issue, two key publications on road safety shed light on, first, the comparison of road safety status between Greece and Norway, and second, on the evaluation of the driving factors in depression.

This publication begins, in Chapter 1, with investigating the predictors of intimate partner violence against women in a sub-Saharan country experiencing a booming alcohol industry. In Chapter 2, the crucial topic of sexual victimization of a vulnerable group in Greek prisons is discussed by presenting findings from a recent research. In Chapter 3, the prediction of a history of arrest in men who perpetrate intimate partner violence is covered using non-linear neural network models. The 4th chapter was written to capture the findings from an exciting community-based project to create a more welcoming and safe community for all members, especially more vulnerable members such as those with dementia and/or an intellectual disability. The next contribution, in Chapter 5, is a cross-cultural study which compares road safety culture among private and professional drivers in significantly different contexts in Norway and in Greece. In Chapter 6, the focus shifts on data resulting from a driver simulator experiment in Greece evaluating driving performance in depression between patients and healthy drivers.

We hope this work will be of assistance to the intended audience (researchers and policy makers) to spur future research and best practices in the respective areas covered.

Joannes Chliaoutakis
Special Issue Editor

Article

Alcohol Drinking by Husbands/Partners Is Associated with Higher Intimate Partner Violence against Women in Angola

Sanni Yaya * and Bishwajit Ghose *

Faculty of Social Sciences, School of International Development and Global Studies, University of Ottawa, Ottawa, ON K1N6N5, Canada
* Correspondence: Sanni.yaya@uottawa.ca (S.Y.); brammaputram@gmail.com (B.G.)

Received: 5 December 2018; Accepted: 15 January 2019; Published: 22 January 2019

Abstract: Intimate partner violence (IPV), as the most prevalent form of violence against women, is a commonly encountered phenomenon across sub-Saharan African countries, including Angola. As a fast-growing economy, Angola is experiencing a booming alcohol industry and persistent IPV and women's rights issues, along with weak prohibition and enforcement against this practice. However, so far, there is no systematic research investigating the predictors of IPV in Angola and whether spousal alcohol drinking has any relationship with women's experience of IPV. Therefore, in this study, we aimed to assess the predictors of IPV (defined as physical, emotional, and sexual violence) among Angolan women with a special focus on their partners' alcohol drinking habit. Cross-sectional data on 7669 women aged 15–49 years from the Angola Demographic and Health Survey were used for this study. Data were analyzed using descriptive and logistic regression methods. Results indicated that physical IPV (32.3%, 95% Confidence Interval = 30.3 to 34.5) was most prevalent, followed by emotional (27.3%, 95% CI = 25.3 to 29.4) and sexual IPV (7.4%, 95% CI = 6.6 to 8.4). In the multivariate analysis, higher education and household wealth status showed protective effects against certain forms of IPV. Alcohol drinking by husbands/partners was associated with significantly higher odds of experiencing physical [OR = 2.950; 95% CI = 2.632, 3.306], emotional [OR = 2.470; 95% CI = 2.187,2.789], and sexual IPV [OR = 2.729; 95% CI = 2.220, 3.354] among women. Women who reported experiencing physical IPV had increased odds of drinking alcohol [OR = 1.474; 95% CI = 1.290, 1.684] compared with those who did not. These findings reflect the widespread prevalence of IPV in sub-Saharan African countries. Special focus should be given to married men with alcohol drinking habits to reduce women's vulnerability to IPV and dependence on alcohol use.

Keywords: Angola; alcohol drinking; intimate partner violence; women's health

1. Introduction

Although historically regarded as a familial issue, IPV has been gaining increasing attention from human rights, health, and social researchers, especially since the Declaration on the Elimination of Violence against Women by United Nations General Assembly in 1993. Violence against women (VAW) is a global phenomenon but is known to be particularly widespread across sub-Saharan Africa (SSA), where it is considered as a major public health, social, and human development challenge at large [1–5]. IPV, which is the most common form of VAW, affects millions of women irrespective of geography, age, sociocultural background, and sexual orientation [2,6]. According to a UN-HABITAT report, (State of the World's Cities, 2006–2007), violence makes up at least 25%–30% of urban crime, including IPV, with the prevalence being twice as high in the developing countries [7]. Intuitively, persistent exposure to torturous and violent behavior by an intimate partner can force a woman to escape from home, resulting in homelessness, economic insecurity, and substance abuse [8–11], which themselves are strong risk factors for abduction, harassment, sexual assault, and socioeconomic marginalization. As such, IPV can have serious repercussions on women's livelihood and economic security, safety, health, and overall well-being [12–15]. Despite this, there is currently no research evidence on IPV in many countries in SSA, including Angola.

To date, a substantial volume of empirical research has been dedicated to exploring the determinants of IPV in SSA. A majority of the studies have interpreted the factors associated with IPV from various demographic, environmental, sociocultural, economic, and interpersonal relational perspectives [1,16–20]. In recent years, a growing number of studies have shown the role of substance abuse, such as problem drinking, on abusive behavior [21–25]. Alcohol drinking is not a predominant cause of IPV, and neither is IPV unknown among men who do not drink. The mechanism through which alcohol use, especially hazardous drinking, can trigger violent behavior is via its role in reducing self-control and increasing proneness to aggression, especially within conjugal relationships [26–28]. There are no country-representative studies on alcohol drinking habit among Angolan men, but some reports maintain that Angola ranks among the top alcohol drinkers in Africa [29]. As the country still struggles to recover from the social disorders left by decades of civil war, the high dependence on alcohol and the occurrence of IPV are supposed be widely prevalent as well due to their overlapping sociopolitical mechanisms.

In the current literature, not much is known regarding the alcohol–IPV relationship in Angola, especially on a nationally representative sample. In addition, most of the past research on substance abuse defined IPV in terms of physical violence, with relatively less attention on other equally important types of violence, including emotional and sexual violence. To this end, we undertook the present study based on recent data from the Angola Demographic and Health Survey (ADHS 2015–2016). The survey, which was nationally representative, interviewed married women aged 15–49 years to collect information on a range of demographic, health, and IPV-related topics. In view of the lack of research evidence on IPV in Angola, we used this open-access data with the objectives of investigating the prevalence and sociocultural predictors of IPV. We also explored the relationship between experiencing IPV and alcohol drinking among women. As we were interested in IPV perpetrated by husbands/partners, we analyzed data only on married women and with a special focus on partners' characteristics, including education and alcohol drinking habits.

2. Methods

2.1. Data Source

This study was based on the Angola Demographic and Health Survey (DHS) conducted in 2015–2016. This is the first standard DHS survey that was conducted in Angola as part of the National Development Strategy Program as well as the Millennium Development Goals. The survey was conducted and coordinated by Instituto Nacional de Estatística in collaboration with the Ministry of Health (Ministério da Saúde or MINSA), along with technical assistance from UNICEF and ICF International through the Demographic and Health Surveys Program and the World Health Organization. The survey collected data on a nationally representative sample, including both urban and rural areas, on a range of demographic and health indicators, such as maternal healthcare use status, fertility, and child mortality rates. For sample selection, a multistage sampling technique was employed involving the systematic selection of clusters at the national level, and the final selection of households from those clusters for survey. Data collection took place from October 2015 to March 2016. In total, 14,975 women were finally interviewed, generating a response rate of 96%. However, the sample population selected for the domestic violence questionnaire was smaller ($n = 7669$) than the entire sample. Details of the survey are available at Instituto Nacional de Estatística (INE), Ministério da Saúde (MINSA), Ministério do Planeamento e do Desenvolvimento Territorial (MINPLAN) e ICF. 2017. Inquérito de Indicadores Múltiplos e de Saúde em Angola 2015–2016. Luanda, Angola e Rockville, Maryland, EUA: INE, MINSA, MINPLAN e ICF.

2.2. Measures

The outcome measure was self-reported experience of abusive behavior/actions perpetrated by husband/partner. The Angola Demographic and Health Survey included a range of questions pertinent to physical, emotional, and sexual assaults. These single-item questions are widely used in assessing self-reported experience of IPV. The following eight items were used for assessing physical abuse: Have you (1) ever been pushed/shook/thrown something; (2) ever been slapped; (3) ever been punched/hit by something; (4) ever been kicked; (5) ever had arm twisted; (6) ever had bruise because of husband's actions, (7) ever had injuries, sprains, dislocation, burns; and (8) ever had wound, broken bones. Emotional abuse was assessed by the following questions: Have you (1) ever been humiliated by husband/partner; (2) ever been threatened with harm by husband/partner; (3) ever been insulted or made to feel bad by husband/partner; and (4) ever experienced any other emotional violence. For sexual abuse, the following two questions were asked: Have you (1) ever forced into unwanted sex and (2) ever experienced other unwanted sexual acts. The answers were categorized as "Yes" if the respondents had ever experienced the given situation and "No" if they have not.

A set of sociodemographic and economic predictor variables were included in the analysis based on their conceptual association with experience of abusive behavior. This was facilitated by a review of the existing literature in other countries in sub-Saharan Africa, including the Democratic Republic of Congo [30], Ethiopia [31], Ghana [32], and Nigeria [33]. The underlying theme that emerged from the review was that women's susceptibility to IPV generally results from low empowerment, such as lower socioeconomic status, as well as behavioral factors embedded in the sociocultural environment, such as ethnic norms, religious guidelines, power relationship in the household (head, wife), and risk factors of abusive behavior (alcohol drinking). In light of this understanding, and depending on availability from the survey dataset, the following were included in the analysis: age groups (15–19/20–24/25–29/30–34/35–39/40–44/45–49); residency (urban/rural); education (no education/completed primary education/completed secondary education/completed higher education); occupation (unemployed/white collar/blue collar); drinks alcohol (no/yes); household head's sex (male/female); wealth status (poorest/richest); husband/partner's education (none/primary/secondary/higher); husband/partner's occupation (unemployed/white collar/blue collar); husband/partner drinks alcohol (no/yes); age difference (0–5 years/6–10 years/>10 years). Description of these variables is provided in Table 1.

Table 1. Sample characteristics. (n = 7669).

Variables	Description	n	%
Age groups			
15–19		619	8.1
20–24		1613	21.0
25–29		1713	22.3
30–34	Age of the respondent in the interview year	1323	17.3
35–39		1036	13.5
40–44		817	10.7
45–49		548	7.1
Residency			
Urban	Whether the respondent is a rural or urban resident	4343	56.6
Rural		3326	43.4
Education			
No Education		2612	34.1
Complete Primary	Highest level of formal education attained by the respondent	2896	37.8
Complete Secondary		1965	25.6
Higher		196	2.6

Table 1. Cont.

Variables	Description	n	%
Occupation			
Unemployed	White collar jobs referred to professional, service, skilled	2046	26.7
White collar	employments. Blue collar included agriculture, clerk, sales,	2580	33.6
Blue collar	and unskilled employments.	3043	39.7
Drinks alcohol			
No	Self-reported drinking habit of the respondent	5917	77.2
Yes		1752	22.8
Household head's sex			
Male	Sex of the person responsible for managing the household	5226	68.1
Female	and making key decisions	2443	31.9
Household wealth quintile	Index of relative wealth status of households based on the		
Poorest (Q1)	possession of durable goods (e.g., refrigerator and TV) and	2914	20.27
Poorer (Q2)	building material (e.g., concrete and wooden), rather than	3367	23.42
Middle (Q3)	personal income [34]. Q1 represents the lowest and Q5 the	3412	23.73
Richer (Q4)	highest wealth quintile.	2526	17.57
Richest (Q5)		2160	15.02
Husband/partner's education			
No Education		1111	16.7
Primary	Highest level of formal education attained by the respondent	1788	26.9
Secondary		2746	41.3
Higher		1002	15.1
Husband/partner's occupation			
Unemployed	White collar jobs referred to professional, service, skilled	574	8.6
White collar	employments. Blue collar included agriculture, clerk, sales,	2911	43.8
Blue collar	and unskilled employments.	3162	47.6
Husband/partner's drinks alcohol			
No	Self-reported drinking habit of the respondent's	4636	60.5
Yes	husband/partner	3033	39.5
Age difference with spouse			
0–5 years	Absolute age difference between respondent and	3445	51.8
6–10 years	respondent's husband/partner	1825	27.5
>10 years		1377	20.7

2.3. Analytical Procedure

All analyses were carried out using StataCorp 14, Texas, USA. The dataset was first scanned for outliers and missing values. Participants who were not selected for the domestic violence module were removed from the analysis. As the survey used cluster survey design, we used the survey design method for all analyses to account for the sampling strata, primary sampling unit, and sampling weight provided in the dataset.

We also ran collinearity tests to check for multicollinearity issues. Only women's alcohol drinking was found to be significantly correlated with age and educational status. At the first step of the analysis, we presented the basic sociodemographic characteristics of the participants in terms of frequencies and percentages. Following that, the prevalence of three different types of IPV (physical, emotional, and sexual) and their individual components were presented as percentages and 95% CIs. At the last step, we conducted multivariate logistic regression to measure the odds of association between the types of IPV and the sociodemographic predictors. To facilitate the selection of the suitable variables, we carried out chi-squared bivariate tests to check which variables were associated with the outcome measures at a significance level of 25%. These were not shown in the results. All the variables met this criterion and were retained for final regression models. Women's alcohol drinking was not included in the regression analysis due to multicollinearity issues.

In total, four models were run: one for experiencing each of the three individual types of IPV and another for experiencing any IPV. Next, we ran four additional regression models to calculate the association between women's alcohol drinking (as outcome measure) and three types of IPV plus any IPV. The four models were designed to adjust the analysis for the sociodemographic variables in certain combinations. The results of regression analysis were presented as odds ratios along with their 95% CIs. A p-value of <0.05 was considered statistically significant for all regression models.

2.4. Ethical Approval

All participants gave informed consent prior to taking part in the interviews. Data were open-access and available online in anonymized form; therefore, no additional approval was necessary.

3. Results

3.1. Descriptive Analysis

In total, 7669 women were included in the analysis. The mean age was 27.65 years (Standard Deviation 9.25), with a greater proportion aged below 30 years. The basic sociodemographic characteristics of the participants are presented in Table 1.

3.2. Prevalence of IPV

The prevalence of three different types of IPV is presented in Table 2. About one-third of the women reported experiencing any physical IPV (32.3%, 95% CI = 30.3 to 34.5), more than a quarter reported any emotional IPV (27.3%, 95% CI = 25.3 to 29.4), and less than one-tenth reported sexual IPV (7.4%, 95% CI = 6.6 to 8.4). Overall, more than two-fifth of the women reported experiencing any IPV (41.1%, 95% CI = 38.7 to 43.6).

Table 2. Prevalence of different forms of intimate partner violence (IPV).

Physical IPV	Never	Often/Sometimes
Pushed/shook/thrown something	88.5 (87.4, 89.6)	11.5 (10.4, 12.6)
Slap	70.5 (68.5, 72.4)	29.5 (27.6, 31.5)
Punch/hit by something	88.6 (87.4, 89.7)	11.4 (10.3, 12.6)
Kick	89.1 (88.0, 90.2)	10.9 (9.8, 12.0)
Arm twisted	90.1 (89.0, 91.2)	9.9 (8.8, 11.0)
Ever had bruise because of husband/partner's actions	69.8 (66.8, 72.6)	30.2 (27.4, 33.2)
Injuries, sprains, dislocation, burns	79.8 (77.0, 82.2)	20.2 (17.8, 23.0)
Wound, broken bones	89.6 (87.4, 91.4)	10.4 (8.6, 12.6)
Any physical IPV	67.7 (65.5, 69.7)	32.3 (30.3, 34.5)
Emotional IPV		
Ever humiliated	84.2 (82.7, 85.5)	15.8 (14.5, 17.3)
Threatened with harm	92.6 (91.6, 93.5)	7.4 (6.5, 8.4)
Insulted/made feel bad	78.8 (76.7, 80.7)	21.2 (19.3, 23.3)
Other emotional violence	72.7 (70.6, 74.7)	27.3 (25.3, 29.4)
Any emotional IPV	72.7 (70.6, 4.7)	27.3 (25.3, 29.4)
Sexual IPV		
Forced into unwanted sex	93.3 (92.5, 94.1)	6.7 (5.9, 7.5)
Other unwanted sexual acts	97.0 (96.3, 97.5)	3.0 (2.5, 3.7)
Any sexual IPV	92.6 (91.6, 93.4)	7.4 (6.6, 8.4)
Any IPV	58.9 (56.4, 61.3)	41.1 (38.7, 43.6)

3.3. Multivariable Analysis

Predictors of experiencing IPV are presented in Table 3. The results revealed that age was not associated with sexual IPV, with women in the higher age groups (e.g., 30–34 years) having relatively lowers odds compared with those in the lowest age group (15–19 years). Women in the rural areas had significantly lower odds of reporting all three types of IPV. Women with higher education were less likely to experience IPV compared with those with no education (except for those in the highest education category). Women in the higher wealth quintile households in general had lower odds of experiencing physical and sexual IPV. The odds of physical IPV in the highest wealth quintile was 0.696 times [95% CI = 0.510, 0.950] lower compared with those in the lowest quintile. Women engaged in blue collar profession had 1.182 times [95% CI = 1.029, 1.358] higher odds of experiencing any form of IPV. The odds of experiencing physical IPV was lower for the female-headed households [OR = 0.832, 95% CI = 0.723, 0.958]. Regarding husband/partner's characteristics, having primary level education was associated with higher odds of physical and emotional IPV. Husband/partner's blue- and white-collar professions were associated with higher odds of sexual and emotional IPV. Alcohol drinking was significantly associated with higher odds of physical [OR = 2.950; 95% CI = 2.632, 3.306], emotional [OR = 2.470; 95% CI = 2.187, 2.789] and sexual [OR = 2.729; 95% CI = 2.220, 3.354] IPV. Having an age gap of 6–10 years showed a protective effect against experiencing IPV [OR = 0.848, 95% CI = 0.746, 0.965].

Table 3. Predictors of different forms of IPV. Angola Demographic and Health Survey (ADHS) 2015.

Variables	Physical IPV	Emotional IPV	Sexual IPV	Any IPV
Age (15–19)				
20–24	1.115	1.212	1.280	1.259
	(0.894, 1.390)	(0.948, 1.548)	(0.869, 1.884)	(0.919, 1.555)
25–29	0.956	1.238	1.085	1.138
	(0.764, 1.198)	(0.966, 1.586)	(0.729, 1.614)	(0.918, 1.410)
30–34	0.903	1.047	0.825	0.947
	(0.712, 1.145)	(0.806, 1.361)	(0.537, 1.267)	(0.754, 1.188)
35–39	0.820	0.971	0.571 *	0.891
	(0.639, 1.052)	(0.738, 1.277)	(0.354, 0.919)	(0.703, 1.130)
40–44	0.842	1.019	0.604 *	0.911
	(0.647, 1.095)	(0.764, 1.359)	(0.365, 0.997)	(0.709, 1.171)
45–49	0.924	1.023	0.613	0.983
	(0.688, 1.242)	(0.739, 1.414)	(0.344, 1.094)	(0.741, 1.305)
Residency (Urban)				
Rural	0.745 ***	0.711 ***	0.665 **	0.781 **
	(0.630, 0.882)	(0.593, 0.854)	(0.495, 0.894)	(0.665, 0.918)
Education (None)				
Complete Primary	0.714 *	0.767	0.725	0.683 **
	(0.548, 0.930)	(0.574, 1.025)	(0.443, 1.186)	(0.530, 0.881)
Complete secondary	0.742 **	0.961	1.073	0.782 *
	(0.610, 0.904)	(0.779, 1.186)	(0.765, 1.507)	(0.648, 0.944)
Secondary	0.558 ***	0.804	0.612	0.625 **
	(0.407, 0.764)	(0.580, 1.114)	(0.326, 1.147)	(0.467, 0.838)
Higher	0.652	0.976	0.863	0.789
	(0.420, 1.014)	(0.625, 1.522)	(0.373, 1.996)	(0.525, 1.186)
Wealth quintile (Q1)				
Poorer	0.967	0.886	1.061	0.920
	(0.817, 1.144)	(0.738, 1.063)	(0.781, 1.442)	(0.784, 1.080)
Middle	0.924	0.768 *	0.747	0.878
	(0.739, 1.156)	(0.603, 0.979)	(0.500, 1.116)	(0.708, 1.087)
Richer	0.862	0.683 **	0.675	0.856
	(0.662, 1.122)	(0.514, 0.908)	(0.423, 1.077)	(0.665, 1.103)
Richest (Q5)	0.696 *	0.782	0.584	0.835
	(0.510, 0.950)	(0.564, 1.084)	(0.333, 1.024)	(0.622, 1.121)

Table 3. Cont.

Variables	Physical IPV	Emotional IPV	Sexual IPV	Any IPV
Occupation (None)				
Blue-collar	1.110	1.151	1.133	1.182 *
	(0.960, 1.283)	(0.986, 1.343)	(0.879, 1.460)	(1.029, 1.358)
White-collar	0.969	1.030	1.016	1.011
	(0.819, 1.146)	(0.859, 1.236)	(0.753, 1.370)	(0.861, 1.187)
Household head's sex (Male)				
Female	0.832 *	0.864	0.916	0.856 *
	(0.723, 0.958)	(0.743, 1.005)	(0.712, 1.179)	(0.749, 0.978)
Husband/Partner's characteristics				
Education (None)				
Complete Primary	1.333 **	1.452 ***	1.104	1.490 ***
	(1.111, 1.600)	(1.190, 1.772)	(0.796, 1.532)	(1.251, 1.774)
Complete secondary	1.209	1.227	0.968	1.259 *
	(0.994, 1.471)	(0.990, 1.521)	(0.681, 1.375)	(1.044, 1.518)
Secondary	1.083	1.046	0.721	1.091
	(0.768, 1.527)	(0.729, 1.501)	(0.373, 1.396)	(0.791, 1.504)
Higher	1.046	0.987	1.133	1.025
	(0.825, 1.325)	(0.758, 1.285)	(0.750, 1.710)	(0.817, 1.286)
Occupation (None)				
Blue-collar	1.171	1.742 ***	1.834 **	1.345 **
	(0.949, 1.446)	(1.363, 2.227)	(1.194, 2.815)	(1.098, 1.647)
White-collar	1.162	1.579 ***	1.601 *	1.265 *
	(0.933, 1.447)	(1.223, 2.039)	(1.025, 2.500)	(1.024, 1.561)
Drinks alcohol (No)				
Yes	2.950 ***	2.470 ***	2.729 ***	2.942 ***
	(2.632, 3.306)	(2.187, 2.789)	(2.220, 3.354)	(2.637, 3.283)
Age difference with spouse (0–5 years)				
6–10	0.848 *	0.959	0.895	0.908
	(0.746, 0.965)	(0.836, 1.099)	(0.710, 1.127)	(0.803, 1.026)
>10	0.912	0.973	1.042	0.923
	(0.789, 1.055)	(0.832, 1.138)	(0.805, 1.348)	(0.803, 1.060)
N	6647	6647	6647	6647

Exponentiated coefficients; 95% confidence intervals in brackets. * $p < 0.05$, ** $p < 0.01$, *** $p < 0.001$.

We ran four additional models to investigate whether or not women who reported experiencing IPV were more or less likely to report drinking alcohol (Table 4). At first, we ran univariate models without adjusting for any covariate and found that only physical IPV was associated with significantly higher odds of drinking alcohol [OR = 1.810, 95% CI = 1.447, 2.264]. This association slightly diminished on progressive adjustment for the individual and husband/partner's characteristics but remained statistically significant. Apart from physical IPV, experiencing any IPV also increased the odds of alcohol [OR = 1.341, 95% CI = 1.177, 1.529].

Model 1 = univariate, Model 2 = Model 1 + women's characteristics, Model 3 = husband/partner's characteristics, Model 4 = women's characteristics + husband/partner's characteristics + age difference.

Table 4. Odds of women's alcohol drinking habit in relation to experiencing any IPV. Angola DHS 2015.

Type of IPV	Model 1	Model 2	Model 3	Model 4
Physical (No)				
Yes	1.810 ***	1.444 **	1.827 ***	1.474 ***
	(1.447, 2.264)	(1.117, 1.867)	(1.456, 2.293)	(1.290, 1.684)
Emotional (No)				
Yes	1.112	0.967	1.078	1.128
	(0.940, 1.315)	(0.797, 1.172)	(0.909, 1.277)	(0.978, 1.300)
Sexual (No)				
Yes	1.017	0.942	1.082	1.185
	(0.831, 1.245)	(0.745, 1.192)	(0.882, 1.329)	(0.943, 1.491)
Any IPV (No)				
Yes	1.045	0.995	1.054	1.341 ***
	(0.805, 1.357)	(0.738, 1.343)	(0.809, 1.374)	(1.177, 1.529)

Exponentiated coefficients; 95% confidence intervals in brackets. * $p < 0.05$, ** $p < 0.01$, *** $p < 0.001$.

4. Discussion

Physical or sexual violence affects more than one-third of all women globally, with adverse physical and psychosocial consequences in the long run [35]. Women experiencing IPV are more prone to injury, depression, unintended pregnancy, and sexually transmitted infections and are almost twice as likely as other women to be alcohol abusers [35]. As such, IPV is a particular concern for women's health in low-income settings because of the inadequate health infrastructure and underappreciation of women's health issues, such as in Angola. In the current study, more than 40% of the women reported experiencing some form of IPV, with more than one-third reporting some form of physical violence. This is higher than previous reports from Malawi (13%–20%) [36], Kenya (37%) [18], South Africa (>20%) [1], and Uganda (36.6%) [37]. However, a Nigerian subnational study among civil servants found a far higher prevalence during the last 12 months (66%) [38]. The large cross-country differences may be explained by the contextual sociocultural factors and by methodological heterogeneity. In this study, we included a generous set of indicators that can be considered as violent actions and behaviors with adverse effects on women's physical and mental health, which might well be the reason behind the higher prevalence of IPV than in most countries for which data are available.

IPV is generally defined as a multifaceted issue with diverse aetiological factors and embedded predominantly into the sociocultural value system determining women's susceptibility to violence and aggression. Sociocultural factors are by far the most commonly cited issues associated with higher degrees of exposure to IPV [17,26,38]. A review of the current literature suggests that the central mechanism through which these factors affect IPV is their impact on women's socioeconomic empowerment. From this perspective, our findings are in line with the existing evidence base. We observed that women with higher educational status generally had lower odds of reporting physical IPV. Higher household wealth status showed an inverse association with sexual IPV, indicating potentially higher sexual autonomy among women in the more well-off households. Surprisingly, women's occupational status did not show any noticeable effect on their experience of IPV but that of their husband/partner did. In general, husband/partner's higher education (completed primary) and better occupational status showed a positive association with IPV. This finding is counterintuitive in the sense that higher socioeconomic status (SES) among husbands/partners has no protective effect on committing spousal violence. This might be indicative of the fact that higher socioeconomic disparity between spouses can increase the likelihood of experiencing IPV. Women in rural areas were less likely to report any form of IPV; this is perhaps linked to lower awareness of the issue and socioeconomic position, which leads to greater acceptance of, or favorable attitude to abusive behavior.

Apart from the socioeconomic factors, the findings also suggest that husband/partner's alcohol drinking can significantly increase the odds of experiencing all forms of IPV. In fact, the strength of the association was highest for husband/partner's alcohol drinking among all the predictor variables. Intuitively, discordant drinking habits can increase relationship stress, decrease marital satisfaction, and increase perpetration of abusive actions [39–41]. Immoderate drinking behavior can lead to increased risk and severity of abusive behavior and initiation and escalation of intimate partner violence (IPV) [42]. These theories are supported by previous multicountry studies in sub-Saharan Africa that found a robust association between husband/partner's alcohol drinking and occurrence of IPV.

A subnational study in South Africa found that about two-third (65%) of the women experiencing spousal abuse reported that their partner was drunk prior to the abusive actions [43]. However, the present findings need to be interpreted with caution as we had no information regarding the level of drinking. Our findings also indicate that women who report physical IPV are more likely to use alcohol than those who do not. The use of alcohol as a destressing mechanism is well known in the medical literature. Experiencing IPV is both physically and psychologically stressful, which in turn increases the likelihood of alcohol consumption as a general coping strategy [44]. Moreover, stressful events evoke thoughts about alcohol and enhances the rewarding effects among those who use it to cope with the negative circumstances [45]. Currently, not much is known about the prevalence of alcohol use in Angola. Therefore, it is suggested that health and social policy-makers take steps to control alcohol consumption as a strategy to reduce the burden of IPV. More studies should be carried out by including the sociocultural predictors of alcohol use and its relationship to IPV in the population.

This is the first study to report the prevalence and predictors of IPV against women in Angola. The data were of good quality and extracted from a nationally representative survey. We applied rigorous methodological and analytical standards and interpreted the findings from two important perspectives: women's empowerment and husband/partner's alcohol drinking behavior. The findings can be of critical importance for taking evidence-based steps to address IPV and focusing on women's empowerment programs in the country. Apart from its important contributions, our study has several important limitations. Firstly, the variables were self-reported and thus remain subject to reporting bias. Secondly, the survey was cross-sectional, hence the associations do not indicate any causal relationship. In addition, the association between husband/partner's alcohol drinking and IPV should be interpreted in light of the fact that we were unable to measure the level of drinking. In many societies, some degree of drinking is acceptable depending on the local context and may not result in loss of self-control to the point that can trigger abusive behavior. Moreover, abusive behavior can be determined to a great extent by the quality of relationship influenced by a variety of complex issues, such as marital satisfaction and household issues that are not necessarily associated with drinking behavior. Future studies should focus on exploring the relational nuances that may explain the mechanism between husband/partner's drinking habit and women's experience of IPV.

5. Conclusions

More than two-third of women aged 15–49 in Angola reported experiencing some form of IPV. Regarding women's characteristics, being residents of rural areas and having higher education were associated with lower likelihood of reporting IPV. Based on this finding, it is suggested that women living in urban areas and lacking schooling experience be given special attention by women's human rights and empowerment programs in an effort to address IPV in Angola. Although the results cannot confirm any causality, it is assumed that husband/partner's alcohol drinking significantly increases the likelihood of IPV. Women reporting IPV were also more likely to use alcohol compared with those who did not. More studies are necessary to investigate the cultural norms that tend to normalize IPV, as well as the dynamics of how alcohol drinking among men contributes to this harmful social practice, in order to design effective intervention approaches. Future studies should also focus on assessing qualitatively whether the amount of alcohol consumed (e.g., social vs. problem drinking) makes any difference in women's experience of IPV.

Author Contributions: Conceptualisation and data acquisition B.G., Analysis: S.Y., B.G.; Interpretation and supervision: S.Y., B.G.; Manuscript writing: B.G.; Final Validation: S.Y., B.G.

Funding: Self-Funded by Bishwajit Ghose.

Acknowledgments: Authors acknowledge the generous provision of the dataset by DHS that made this study possible.

Conflicts of Interest: The authors declare no conflict of interest.

Abbreviations

ADHS 2015	Angola Demographic and Health Survey
SSA	sub-Saharan Africa
IPV	intimate partner violence
VAW	violence against women

References

1. Groves, A.K.; Moodley, D.; McNaughton-Reyes, L.; Martin, S.L.; Foshee, V.; Maman, S. Prevalence and rates of intimate partner violence among South African women during pregnancy and the postpartum period. *Mater. Child Health J.* **2015**, *19*, 487–495. [CrossRef]
2. Stark, L.; Asghar, K.; Yu, G.; Bora, C.; Baysa, A.A.; Falb, K.L. Prevalence and associated risk factors of violence against conflict–affected female adolescents: A multi–country, cross–sectional study. *J. Glob. Health* **2017**. [CrossRef]
3. Adedini, S.A.; Odimegwu, C.; Bamiwuye, O.; Fadeyibi, O.; de Wet, N. Barriers to accessing health care in Nigeria: Implications for child survival. *Glob. Health Act.* **2014**, *7*. [CrossRef]
4. Garcia-Moreno, C.; Watts, C. Violence against women: An urgent public health priority. *Bull. World Health Organ.* **2011**, *89*, 2. [CrossRef]
5. Dalal, S.; Johnson, C.; Fonner, V.; Kennedy, C.E.; Siegfried, N.; Figueroa, C.; Baggaley, R. Improving HIV test uptake and case finding with assisted partner notification services. *AIDS* **2017**, *31*, 1867–1876. [CrossRef]
6. Chibber, K.S.; Krishnan, S. Confronting intimate partner violence, a global health care prioitity. *Mt. Sin. J. Med.* **2011**, *78*, 449–457. [CrossRef]
7. UN-HABITAT. Gender I Women's Safety and Security in Cities. Available online: http://mirror.unhabitat.org/content.asp?typeid=19&catid=303&cid=6849 (accessed on 20 November 2018).
8. Eisenman, D.P.; Richardson, E.; Sumner, L.A.; Ahmad, S.R.; Liu, H.; Valentine, J.; Rodriguez, M.A. Intimate Partner Violence and Community Service Needs among Pregnant and Post-partum Latina Women. *Viol. Vict.* **2009**, *24*, 111–121. [CrossRef]
9. Nyamathi, A.; Marfisee, M.; Zhang, S.; Hall, E.; Farabee, D.; Marfisee, M.; Khalilifard, F.; Faucette, M.; Leake, B. Correlates of Serious Violent Crime for Recently Released Parolees with a History of Homelessness. *Viol. Vict.* **2012**, *27*, 793–810. [CrossRef]
10. Gerassi, L. From Exploitation to Industry: Definitions, Risks, and Consequences of Domestic Sexual Exploitation and Sex Work Among Women and Girls. *J. Hum. Behav. Soc. Environ.* **2015**, *25*, 591–605. [CrossRef]
11. Montesanti, S.R.; Thurston, W.E. Mapping the role of structural and interpersonal violence in the lives of women: Implications for public health interventions and policy. *BMC Womens Health* **2015**, *15*. [CrossRef]
12. Antai, D.; Adaji, S. Community-level influences on women's experience of intimate partner violence and terminated pregnancy in Nigeria: A multilevel analysis. *BMC Preg. Child.* **2012**, *12*, 128. [CrossRef]
13. Colombini, M.; Dockerty, C.; Mayhew, S.H. Barriers and Facilitators to Integrating Health Service Responses to Intimate Partner Violence in Low- and Middle-Income Countries: A Comparative Health Systems and Service Analysis. *Stud. Fam. Plan.* **2017**, *48*, 179–200. [CrossRef]
14. Joyner, K.; Mash, R.J. The value of intervening for intimate partner violence in South African primary care: Project evaluation. *BMJ Open* **2011**, *1*. [CrossRef]

15. Medie, P.A. Women and Postconflict Security: A Study of Police Response to Domestic Violence in Liberia. *Politics Gender* **2015**, *11*, 478–498. [CrossRef]
16. Gibbs, A.; Carpenter, B.; Crankshaw, T.; Hannass-Hancock, J.; Smit, J.; Tomlinson, M.; Butler, L. Prevalence and factors associated with recent intimate partner violence and relationships between disability and depression in post-partum women in one clinic in eThekwini Municipality, South Africa. *PLoS ONE* **2017**, *12*. [CrossRef]
17. Shamu, S.; Abrahams, N.; Temmerman, M.; Musekiwa, A.; Zarowsky, C. A Systematic Review of African Studies on Intimate Partner Violence against Pregnant Women: Prevalence and Risk Factors. *PLoS ONE* **2011**, *6*. [CrossRef]
18. Makayoto, L.A.; Omolo, J.; Kamweya, A.M.; Harder, V.S.; Mutai, J. Prevalence and Associated Factors of Intimate Partner Violence Among Pregnant Women Attending Kisumu District Hospital, Kenya. *Mater. Child Health J.* **2013**, *17*, 441–447. [CrossRef]
19. Alangea, D.O.; Addo-Lartey, A.A.; Sikweyiya, Y.; Chirwa, E.D.; Coker-Appiah, D.; Jewkes, R.; Adanu, R.A.K. Prevalence and risk factors of intimate partner violence among women in four districts of the central region of Ghana: Baseline findings from a cluster randomised controlled trial. *PLoS ONE* **2018**, *13*, e0200874. [CrossRef]
20. Andarge, E.; Shiferaw, Y. Disparities in Intimate Partner Violence among Currently Married Women from Food Secure and Insecure Urban Households in South Ethiopia: A Community Based Comparative Cross-Sectional Study. *Biomed. Res. Int.* **2018**, *2018*. [CrossRef]
21. Klostermann, K.C. Substance abuse and intimate partner violence: Treatment considerations. *Subst. Abuse Treat. Prev. Policy* **2006**, *1*, 24. [CrossRef]
22. Chermack, S.T.; Murray, R.L.; Winters, J.J.; Walton, M.A.; Booth, B.M.; Blow, F.C. Treatment Needs of Men and Women with Violence Problems in Substance Use Disorder Treatment. *Subst. Use Misuse* **2009**, *44*, 1236–1262. [CrossRef] [PubMed]
23. Golinelli, D.; Longshore, D.; Wenzel, S.L. Substance Use and Intimate Partner Violence: Clarifying the Relevance of Women's Use and Partners' Use. *J. Behav. Health Serv. Res.* **2009**, *36*, 199–211. [CrossRef] [PubMed]
24. Martin, S.L.; Beaumont, J.L.; Kupper, L.L. Substance use before and during pregnancy: Links to intimate partner violence. *Am. J. Drug Alcohol. Abuse* **2003**, *29*, 599–617. [CrossRef] [PubMed]
25. Moore, B.C.; Easton, C.J.; McMahon, T.J. Drug Abuse and Intimate Partner Violence: A Comparative Study of Opioid-Dependent Fathers. *Am. J. Orthopsychiatry* **2011**, *81*, 218–227. [CrossRef] [PubMed]
26. Wilson, I.M.; Graham, K.; Taft, A. Alcohol interventions, alcohol policy and intimate partner violence: A systematic review. *BMC Public Health* **2014**, *14*. [CrossRef]
27. Vieira, L.B.; Cortes, L.F.; de Mello Padoin, S.M.; de Oliveira Souza, I.E.; de Paula, C.C.; Terra, M.G. Abuse of alcohol and drugs and violence against women: Experience reports. *Rev. Bras. Enferm.* **2014**, *67*, 366–372. [CrossRef] [PubMed]
28. Lim, S.S.; Vos, T.; Flaxman, A.D.; Danaei, G.; Shibuya, K.; Adair-Rohani, H.; AlMazroa, M.A.; Amann, M.; Anderson, R.; Andrews, K.G.; et al. A comparative risk assessment of burden of disease and injury attributable to 67 risk factors and risk factor clusters in 21 regions, 1990-2010: A systematic analysis for the Global Burden of Disease Study 2010. *Lancet* **2012**, *380*, 2224–2260. [CrossRef]
29. Mikva, K. 17 Top Alcohol-Drinking Countries in Africa. Moguldom. 2015. Available online: https://moguldom.com/28638/17-top-alcohol-drinking-countries-in-africa/ (accessed on 23 November 2018).
30. Peterman, A.; Palermo, T.; Bredenkamp, C. Estimates and Determinants of Sexual Violence Against Women in the Democratic Republic of Congo. *Am. J. Public Health* **2011**, *101*, 1060–1067. [CrossRef]
31. Fekadu, E.; Yigzaw, G.; Gelaye, K.A.; Ayele, T.A.; Minwuye, T.; Geneta, T.; Teshome, D.F. Prevalence of domestic violence and associated factors among pregnant women attending antenatal care service at University of Gondar Referral Hospital, Northwest Ethiopia. *BMC Womens Health* **2018**, *18*. [CrossRef]
32. Owusu Adjah, E.S.; Agbemafle, I. Determinants of domestic violence against women in Ghana. *BMC Public Health* **2016**, *16*. [CrossRef]
33. Bishwajit, G.; Yaya, S. Domestic violence: A hidden barrier to contraceptive use among women in Nigeria. *Open Access J. Contracept.* **2018**, *9*, 21–28. [CrossRef]
34. Bishwajit, G. Household wealth status and overweight and obesity among adult women in Bangladesh and Nepal. *Obes. Sci. Pract.* **2017**, *3*, 185–192. [CrossRef] [PubMed]

35. WHO | Violence against Women: A 'Global Health Problem of Epidemic Proportions'. Available online: https://www.who.int/mediacentre/news/releases/2013/violence_against_women_20130620/en/ (accessed on 3 December 2018).
36. Bazargan-Hejazi, S.; Medeiros, S.; Mohammadi, R.; Lin, J.; Dalal, K. Patterns of Intimate Partner Violence: A study of female victims in Malawi. *J. Injury Viol. Res.* **2013**, *5*, 38–50. [CrossRef]
37. Osinde, M.O.; Kaye, D.K.; Kakaire, O. Intimate partner violence among women with HIV infection in rural Uganda: Critical implications for policy and practice. *BMC Womens Health* **2011**, *11*, 50. [CrossRef] [PubMed]
38. Adejimi, A.A.; Fawole, O.I.; Sekoni, O.O.; Kyriacou, D.N. Prevalence and Correlates of Intimate Partner Violence among Male Civil Servants in Ibadan, Nigeria. *Afr. J. Med. Sci.* **2014**, *43*, 51–60.
39. Leadley, K.; Clark, C.L.; Caetano, R. Couples' drinking patterns, intimate partner violence, and alcohol-related partnership problems. *J. Subst. Abuse* **2000**, *11*, 253–263. [CrossRef]
40. Homish, G.G.; Leonard, K.E. Marital quality and congruent drinking. *J. Stud. Alcohol.* **2005**, *66*, 488–496. [CrossRef] [PubMed]
41. Homish, G.G.; Leonard, K.E. The drinking partnership and marital satisfaction: The longitudinal influence of discrepant drinking. *J. Consult. Clin. Psychol.* **2007**, *75*, 43–51. [CrossRef]
42. Wilson, I.M.; Graham, K.; Taft, A. Living the cycle of drinking and violence: A qualitative study of women's experience of alcohol-related intimate partner violence: Alcohol-related intimate partner violence. *Drug Alcohol. Rev.* **2017**, *36*, 115–124. [CrossRef]
43. O'Connor, M.J.; Tomlinson, M.; LeRoux, I.M.; Stewart, J.; Greco, E.; Rotheram-Borus, M.J. Predictors of Alcohol Use Prior to Pregnancy Recognition among Township Women in Cape Town, South Africa. *Soc. Sci. Med.* **2011**, *72*, 83–90. [CrossRef]
44. Keyes, K.; Hatzenbuehler, M.; Grant, B.F.; Hasin, D.S. Stress and Alcohol. *Alcohol. Res.* **2012**, *34*, 391–400. [PubMed]
45. Thomas, S.E.; Merrill, J.E.; von Hofe, J.; Magid, V. Coping Motives for Drinking Affect Stress Reactivity but Not Alcohol Consumption in a Clinical Laboratory Setting. *J. Stud. Alcohol. Drugs* **2014**, *75*, 115–123. [CrossRef] [PubMed]

© 2019 by the authors. Licensee MDPI, Basel, Switzerland. This article is an open access article distributed under the terms and conditions of the Creative Commons Attribution (CC BY) license (http://creativecommons.org/licenses/by/4.0/).

Article

Is Sexual Assault a Problem in Greek Prisons? Initial Evidence from a Greek Male Prison

Maria Papadakaki [1,*], Angelos Tsalkanis [2], Dimitra Prokopiadou [3], Martha Goutsou [1] and Joannes Chliaoutakis [1]

[1] Department of Social Work, Hellenic Mediterranean University, 71004 Heraklion, Greece; martgou@yahoo.gr (M.G.); jchlia@staff.teicrete.gr (J.C.)
[2] Department of Social Work, University of West Attica, 12241 Athens, Greece; tsalkanis@gmail.com
[3] Health Care Centre of Arkalochori, 70300 Heraklion Crete, Greece; dprokopiadou@gmail.com
* Correspondence: mpapadakaki@yahoo.gr; Tel.: +30-2810-379-518

Received: 13 September 2019; Accepted: 25 November 2019; Published: 28 November 2019

Abstract: This study aimed to explore the problem of inmate sexual victimization in a Greek male prison. A total of 400 individuals were approached in the largest Greek male prison and 50 individuals participated. The questionnaire examined sociodemographic, offence-related information, sexual victimization during incarceration, experiences of witnessing the sexual coercion of other inmates, and history of sexual victimization. Thirteen (26.0%) participants reported sexual victimization by an inmate, including either "only non-penetrative" or "only penetrative ones" or "both penetrative and non-penetrative" ones. The victimized participants also performed worse in child sexual victimization and self-esteem scores as compared with the non-victimized ones. Vulnerable groups identified in the current study could receive further attention in future studies and policy initiatives. Large-scale surveys could be designed to extend our knowledge on this neglected area of research.

Keywords: sexual assault; coercion; inmates; prison; offence; self-esteem

1. Introduction

It is common for some inmates to trade goods for drugs or even to use sex in order to arrange their debts with other inmates when they lack resources. However, sexual intercourse in prison is not always consensual and for many years sexual assault remains a main problem for prisoners with certain consequences for institutional life. Inmate-on-inmate rape is a serious human rights abuse and a major public health problem. A Human Rights Watch Report [1] identified the huge traumatic effect of male rape on victims' psychology with an emphasis placed on the feelings of shame. A high potential of suicide has also been evident among sexually victimized inmates as a result of desperateness and helplessness. It is also common for inmates to take precautions against sexual assault that render their environment more dangerous, such as launching pre-emptive strikes or joining gangs for protection; some even get injured while defending themselves [2]. Most importantly, there is a public health concern due to the extent that sexual assault contributes to the transmission of HIV among the population of inmates because of unprotected sexual activity [3–5].

1.1. Theoretical Explanations and Prevalence Estimates of Sexual Misconduct in Correctional Settings

Predators in prison ordinarily are primarily heterosexual, but they have been said to sexually assault other male prisoners in an attempt to gain control over those who are weak [6]. On the basis of the conceptual framework of hegemonic masculinity, some argue that male rape reflects society's expectations for men to be forceful and pervasive, with male rape being the worst manifestation of power against the weak through gaining control over their body [7–9].

The importation and the deprivation model have been widely employed as explanatory frameworks of prison violence [10]. On the one hand, the importation model holds an individual inmate's proneness to violence responsible for violence, and underlines the fact that predators have a personal history that explains their inclination to violence. On the other hand, the deprivation model holds environmental factors responsible for violence and suggests that prison life together with forced isolation, traumatize individuals and generate an oppositional prison subculture, promoting violence for self-preservation. In addition, the transactional model introduces another explanation of prison violence, focusing on the dynamic interaction of prisoners' individual characteristics and the prison environment [11].

Sexual assault seems to be very prevalent in prison settings. Most studies typically report a high incidence of sexual aggression (11% to 40%), and a lower incidence of rape (1% to 3%) [12]. However, estimations seem to vary across geographical settings, and this is partly attributed to the variety of methodologies employed in international research. In Australia, 26% of male inmates aged 18 to 25 years reported experiences of sexual assault, and 8% were assaulted weekly or daily [13]. In U.S. state prisons, one in every five male inmates reported experiences of sexual misconduct with 7% being raped [14]. A Bureau of Justice Statistics (BJS) survey identified that 4.5% of federal prisoners were sexually victimized over a period of one year [15]. In 2011, the U.S. National Prison Rape Statistics Program (NIS 3) identified a total of 4.0% of prison inmates and 3.2% of jail inmates that revealed experiences of sexual victimization [16]. A total of 9.6% of former U.S. state prisoners reported sexual victimization during their latest period of incarceration [17]. Apart from Australia and USA, research from other parts of the world on risk factors of victimization is scarce, especially regarding demographic, behavioral health, and criminal parameters [18]. In fact, the first population-based study on male sexual misconduct in Australia was only published in 2016 [19] while data from Europe are scarce and very local. However, due to the institutional, cultural, and historical differences, USA and Australian findings may not be generalizable to other contexts [19]. A lot of challenges also exist with understanding and recording sexual coercion among juvenile prisoners, and system shortcomings have been recently noticed [20].

1.2. Sexual Misconduct and Human Rights' Protection in the Greek Correctional Settings

Rape and sexual misconduct in prison constitute violations of human rights and they are considered to be acts of torture [21]. At the international level, there are conventions and treaties prohibiting torture (e.g., the Convention against Torture and Other Cruel, Inhuman or Degrading Treatment or Punishment [21] and the International Covenant on Civil and Political Rights [22]), explicitly stating that prisoners, like all citizens, have civil and political rights and should not be subjected to degrading treatment. In 2002, a new system (Convention against Torture, CAT) was introduced for the prevention of torture and ill-treatment in correctional facilities, which involved regular visits by international bodies, for the oversight of prison conditions, as well as the detection of degrading treatment.

Although Greece ratified CAT in 1988 and OPCAT (Optional protocol to the Convention against Torture and Other Cruel, Inhuman or degrading Treatment or punishment) in 2014, the subject of inmates' sexual victimization has not been explored efficiently due to its sensitive nature and, so far, there is no known published data estimating the extent of the problem and its correlates in Greek prisons. There are a few studies on various behaviors of incarcerated sexual offenders [23,24] but none of them have been designed to assess the problem in the general population of Greek inmates. Moreover, there is no database at the national level to monitor the prevalence and the patterns of sexual violence within prison facilities, and therefore the extent of the problem is not precisely known.

The current study comes in a timely manner as the financial crisis and the long recession faced by the Greek economy, since 2008, has greatly affected the conditions of many correctional facilities, while at the same time the number of incoming prisoners have surpassed the governments' ability to manage the new demands. According to the figures of the Council of Europe, overcrowding in Greek prisons has been the worst in EU, with the prison density per 100 places (prisoners in relation to places available) being the highest in the EU [25]. At the same time, the European Court of Human Rights identified three cases of inmates suffering poor detention conditions in Greek prisons in breach of the European Convention on Human Rights [26].

Likewise, the Council of Europe's Committee for the Prevention of Torture and Inhuman or Degrading Treatment or Punishment (CPT) in its biannual reports identified a disastrous situation in many areas of the prison system. The 2012 report published upon the Committee's visit on September 2011 [27], showed Greek prisons overcrowded at 151.7 percent capacity and a number of shortcomings in the Greek prison system (http://www.cpt.coe.int/documents/grc/2012-01-inf-eng.pdf). The situation, since 2011, has showed no improvement. The next report [28] published upon the Committee's visit on April 2013 noted that overcrowding was not efficiently addressed, since most of the prisons still operated at 200% to 300% of their capacity with lack of hygiene and medical screening upon admission, as well as with a shortage of health-care staff (http://www.cpt.coe.int/documents/grc/2014-10-16-eng.htm). Lack of prison staff was emphasized as impeding any effort to monitor prisoners and prevent the violent assaults against vulnerable groups of prisoners.

What is more alarming is the fact that the CPT Committee, both in 2014 and 2016, identified serious deficits in the process of interrogation and the investigation of allegations for ill-treatment and repeatedly recommended a proper internal complaints system accessible at any moment, being confidential, followed by formal investigation, and keeping the prisoner in informed of actions taken (CPT Report March 2016; https://rm.coe.int/168069667e). Despite the Greek Authorities' compliance with the recommendations of the European Committee and the promising measures taken to tackle this problem, there is still uncertainty about the enforcement and the sustainability of these measures in Greece during this critical period of economic crisis. The staff shortages and the salary cuts have severely affected the quality of prison services and the budget cuts have limited the possibility of improvements in prison life. The staff seem to lack rudimentary knowledge and techniques to efficiently cope with difficult situations, while their education has been oriented towards a punishment-based model rather than a model that emphasizes the detainees' integration and psychosocial adjustment. The latest visit of CPT to Greek prisons was conducted in 2019 to review the progress made by the Greek authorities since 2015 in relation to prison matters, but the report has not yet been published (https://www.coe.int/en/web/cpt/-/council-of-europe-anti-torture-committee-visits-prisons-and-police-establishments-in-greece).

Under these circumstances and given the difficulty that has been noted of gaining access to prison populations [29], this study is expected to facilitate the initial assessment of the problem of inmate sexual violence, as well as offer important information for the design of large-scale surveys. Evidence from this study could also enable international comparisons of inmates' needs and the harmonization of future interventions.

2. Materials and Methods

2.1. Sampling

The largest prison in the country, housing approximately half of all the inmates of judicial prisons in the whole country (2000 out of 4500 in total) was selected out of 13 prison facilities that operate in Greece (Greek Ministry of Justice). Immigrants and illiterate inmates were excluded from the study to ensure that all the participants would have an adequate understanding of the study questionnaire. The prisoners' registry was used to identify the immigrants. The staff of the Social Service Department undertook the task of identifying the illiterate inmates based on personal data recorded during consultation with the inmates. A total of 400 inmates fulfilled all the above criteria and were eligible to participate in the study. All the eligible inmates were invited to participate in the study and received a sealed envelope containing an information sheet and a consent form, a questionnaire, and a postage envelope return addressed to the researchers. Informed consent was necessary prior to participation. The information sheet informed the participants about the study objectives and procedures, as well as about the option they had to withdraw from the study at any moment and receive psychological or emotional support, safely, in case they were overwhelmed by negative emotions due to recalling a traumatic experience. Participants returned the questionnaire completed in a sealed mailbox, which was circulated with confidentiality in the various prison sections by a prison social worker and an assistant. This particular social worker was assigned the role of intermediating between prisoners and the research team and had previously received structured guidance by members of the research team regarding their role to emerging queries regarding the nature of the study, as well as their response to alarming emotional reactions during the study implementation.

2.2. Research Instrument

This study used a self-administered questionnaire, which was developed on the basis of international literature [30,31] and was completed anonymously. The questionnaire elicited information on sociodemographic and offence-related characteristics, as well as on the participants' experiences of sexual coercion by an inmate during their incarceration. Two individual questions, with "yes/no" response option, were used to measure sexual victimization during the current incarceration ("Since the time you have been incarcerated in this facility has any of your inmates attempted to kiss or touch any part of your body in a sexually offensive way against your will (touching of genitals, etc.)?" and "Since the time you have been incarcerated in this facility has any of your inmates forced you to a sexual intercourse against your will (oral or anal sex)?"). A positive response to at least one of the two questions implied sexual victimization by an inmate during the current incarceration. Witnessing the sexual coercion of another inmate during the current incarceration was measured through the question "Since the time you have been admitted in this facility have you witnessed an inmate's sexual coercion?" with yes/no response option. Participants' sexual victimization during childhood was captured through a set of six questions with yes/no response option (Did you experience any of the following situations by an individual at least 5 years older than you, when you were 16 years old or younger, which were conducted in a sexual way and were not part of age-appropriate family/parenting interactions? (a) hugs/kisses in a sexual way; (b) display of genitals; (c) touching body parts; (d) touching genitals; (e) attempted anal contact; (f) completed anal contact). A positive response to at least one of the six questions implied sexual victimization during childhood. Participants were further asked to select their preferred response strategies (yes/no option) in a potential sexual victimization among a list of 11 strategies (e.g., violent reaction, disclosure to prison guard, request for cell transfer, do nothing). Lastly, participants' self-esteem was measured through the Rosenberg Self-Esteem Scale [32]. This particular scale has previously demonstrated high reliability in a Greek sample [33,34]. The scale measures the positive or negative view of oneself through 10 individual items. Participants are asked to indicate the extent of their agreement or disagreement with these 10 items on a 4-point scale anchoring from 1 (strongly disagree) to 4 (strongly agree).

3. Results

A total of 50 individuals returned the questionnaire completed out of the 400 individuals that received the questionnaire.

3.1. Participants' Sociodemographic Characteristics

Participants had a mean age of 33.0 years (SD = 8.9). Most of them were single (n = 28, 56.0%), heterosexual (n = 38, 76.0%), graduates of senior high school (n = 30, 60.0%), salaried prior to incarceration (n = 22, 44.0%), and more than half of them had no past penalties (n = 30, 60.0%) (Table 1).

Table 1. Participants' sociodemographic and offence-related characteristics.

n = 50	n	%
Age *	33.0	8.9
Family status		
Married	10	20.0
Single	28	56.0
In separation	6	12.0
Divorced	5	10.0
Widow	1	2.0
Educational level		
Primary school	6	12.0
Junior high school	8	16.0
Senior high school	30	60.0
Higher education	6	12.0
Occupation		
Salaried	22	44.0
Self-employed	13	26.0
Unemployed	9	18.0
Other	6	12.0
Sexual orientation		
Homosexual	4	8.0
Heterosexual	38	76.0
Bisexual	8	16.0
Past conviction		
No past conviction	30	60.0
Past conviction for same offence	13	26.0
Past conviction for other offence	7	14.0

* Mean, Standard Deviation.

3.2. Experiences of Sexual Victimization

A total of thirteen participants (26.0%) were sexually victimized during incarceration as they responded positively to at least one of the two relevant questions. Out of the 13 sexually victimized participants, a total of five participants (38.5%) experienced only non-penetrative sexual victimization (admitted that an inmate attempted to touch them in a sexually offensive way during their current incarceration), one participant (7.7%) experienced only penetrative sexual victimization (forced by an inmate to have oral or anal sexual contact against their will), and seven participants (53.8%) experienced both types of sexual victimization. Detailed information on the experiences of sexual victimization is provided in Tables 2–5.

Table 2. Personal characteristics of the study participants.

Personal Information	No Victimization (n = 37)	Victimization (n = 13)	Sexually Victimized (n = 13)		
			Only Non Penetrative Sexual Victimization (n = 5)	Only Penetrative Sexual Victimization (n = 1)	Both Penetrative and Non-Penetrative (n = 7)
Age *	32.8 (7.8)	31.6 (7.0)	32.02 (7.56)	-	30.2 (8.3)
Family status					
Single	21 (56.7)	7 (53.8)	2 (40.0)	-	5 (71.4)
Married	9 (24.4)	1 (7.7)	1 (20.0)	-	0 (0.0)
In separation	4 (10.8)	2 (15.4)	1 (20.0)	-	0 (0.0)
Divorced	2 (5.4)	3 (23.1)	1 (20.0)	-	2 (28.6)
Widow	1 (2.7)	0 (0.0)	0 (0.0)	-	0 (0.0)
Educational level					
Primary	5 (13.5)	0 (0.0)	0 (0.0)	-	0 (0.0)
Junior high school	5 (13.5)	4 (30.8)	0 (0.0)	-	3 (42.8)
Senior high school	23 (62.2)	7 (53.8)	5 (100.0)	-	2 (28.6)
Higher education	4 (10.8)	2 (15.4)	0 (0.0)	-	2 (28.6)
Occupation					
Salaried	19 (51.3)	3 (23.1)	0 (0.0)	-	3 (42.8)
Self-employed	11 (29.7)	2 (15.4)	1 (20.0)	-	1 (14.2)
Unemployed	4 (10.8)	5 (38.4)	2 (40.0)	-	2 (28.8)
Other	3 (8.2)	3 (23.1)	2 (40.0)	-	1 (14.2)
Sexual orientation					
Homosexual	0 (0.0)	4 (30.8)	1 (20.0)	-	2 (28.6)
Heterosexual	33 (89.2)	5 (38.4)	2 (40.0)	-	3 (42.8)
Bisexual	4 (10.8)	4 (30.8)	2 (40.0)	-	2 (28.6)
Self-esteem *	28.2 (4.8)	27.3 (2.1)	28.2 (1.7)	32.0 (N/A)	26.1 (1.0)

* Mean, Standard Deviation.

Table 3. Offence-related characteristics of the study participants.

Offence-Related Information	No Victimization (n = 37)	Victimization (n = 13)	Sexually Victimized (n = 13)		
			Only Non Penetrative Sexual Victimization (n = 5)	Only Penetrative Sexual Victimization (n = 1)	Both Penetrative and Non-Penetrative (n = 7)
Past conviction					
No	28 (75.7)	2 (15.4)	0 (0.0)	-	2 (28.6)
Yes, same offence	7 (18.9)	6 (46.1)	2 (40.0)	1 (100.0)	3 (42.8)
Yes, other offence	2 (5.4)	5 (38.5)	3 (60.0)	-	2 (28.6)
Current offence					
Robbery	5 (13.5)	4 (30.8)	1 (20.0)	-	3 (42.8)
Theft	3 (8.0)	0 (0.0)	0 (0.0)	-	0 (0.0)
Homicide	5 (13.5)	1 (7.7)	1 (20.0)	-	0 (0.0)
Debts	2 (5.4)	0 (0.0)	0 (0.0)	-	0 (0.0)
Drugs	18 (48.6)	3 (23.0)	2 (40.0)	-	1 (14.2)
Rape/lewdness	0 (0.0)	1 (7.7)	0 (0.0)	-	1 (14.2)
Bawdiness	1 (2.7)	0 (0.0)	0 (0.0)	-	0 (0.0)
Pedophilia	0 (0.0)	2 (15.4)	1 (20.0)	-	1 (14.2)
Pornography	1 (2.7)	1 (7.7)	0 (0.0)	1 (100.0)	0 (0.0)
Other	2 (5.4)	1 (7.7)	0 (0.0)	-	1 (14.2)
Sentence duration					
Life imprisonment	2 (5.4)	1 (7.7)	1 (20.0)	0 (0.0)	0 (0.0)
5–20 years	10 (27.0)	9 (69.3)	3 (60.0)	1 (100.0)	5 (71.4)
10 days–5 years	12 (32.4)	3 (23.0)	1 (20.0)	0 (0.0)	2 (28.6)
1 day–1 month	5 (13.5)	0 (0.0)	0 (0.0)	0 (0.0)	0 (0.0)
Pre-trial detention	1 (2.7)	0 (0.0)	0 (0.0)	0 (0.0)	0 (0.0)

Table 4. Strategies preferred by the study participants in response to potential sexual victimization in prison.

Response Strategies	No Victimization (n = 37)	Victimization (n = 13)	Sexually Victimized (n = 13)		
			Only Non Penetrative Sexual Victimization (n = 5)	Only Penetrative Sexual Victimization (n = 1)	Both Penetrative and Non-Penetrative (n = 7)
Revenge	11 (29.7)	9 (69.3)	4 (80.0)	-	5 (71.4)
Violent reaction	18 (48.6)	9 (69.3)	4 (80.0)	-	5 (71.4)
Disclosure to co-mate	9 (24.3)	5 (38.5)	2 (40.0)	1	2 (28.6)
Disclosure to family	8 (21.6)	3 (23.0)	2 (40.0)	-	1 (14.2)
Disclosure to friends	6 (16.2)	5 (38.5)	2 (40.0)	1	2 (28.6)
Disclosure to head officer	6 (16.2)	4 (30.8)	2 (40.0)	1	1 (14.2)
Disclosure to prison guard	6 (16.2)	2 (15.4)	0 (0.0)	1	1 (14.2)
Disclosure to prison service providers (e.g., doctor)	8 (21.6)	2 (15.4)	0 (0.0)	1	1 (14.2)
Application for cell transfer	19 (51.3)	8 (61.5)	3 (60.0)	-	5 (71.4)
Nothing	3 (8.1)	1 (7.7)	0 (0.0)	-	1 (14.2)
Other	6 (16.2)	3 (23.0)	2 (40.0)	-	1 (14.2)

Table 5. Other sexual victimization experiences of the study participants.

Past Sexual Victimization	No Victimization (n = 37)	Victimization (n = 13)	Sexually Victimized (n = 13)		
			Only Non Penetrative Sexual Victimization (n = 5)	Only Penetrative Sexual Victimization (n = 1)	Both Penetrative and Non-Penetrative (n = 7)
Childhood sexual victimization (<16 years) (situations not part of age-appropriate family/parenting interactions)					
Hugs	9 (24.3)	8 (61.5)	2 (40.0)	1	5 (71.4)
Display of genitals	5 (13.5)	2 (15.4)	1 (20.0)	-	1 (14.2)
Petting	9 (24.3)	9 (69.3)	2 (40.0)	1	6 (85.7)
Touching genitals	7 (18.9)	5 (38.5)	1 (20.0)	1	3 (42.8)
Attempted anal sex	3 (8.1)	4 (30.8)	2 (40.0)	-	2 (28.6)
Completed anal sex	2 (5.4)	4 (30.8)	1 (20.0)	-	3 (42.8)
Total Child sexual victimization (Mean/SD)	1.2 (1.9)	2.5 (2.0)	1.8 (2.4)	3.0 (N/A)	3.0 (1.8)
Witness inmate's sexual victimization					
Yes	7 (18.9)	13 (100.0)	5 (100.0)	1 (100.0)	7 (100.0)

3.3. Victims' Profile

Participants who reported only non-penetrative victimization ($n = 5$) had a mean age of 32.0 years (SD7.56), were mostly single (40.0%) and unemployed (40.0%), graduates of senior high school (100.0%), and many of them were heterosexual and bisexual (40.0% each). The majority of them were currently sentenced for five to 20 years (69.3%), many of them were convicted for drugs (40.0%), and most of them had a past conviction for other offences (60.0%). All of them had witnessed another inmate's sexual victimization during their current incarceration. They had a total score of 1.8 (SD2.4) in child sexual victimization and their self-esteem had an average of 28.2 (SD1.7). Most of them would prefer to react violently and retaliate in response to a potential sexual victimization (80.0%).

There was only one participant who reported only penetrative victimization was currently sentenced for five to 20 years for pornography and had past convictions for the same offences. He had witnessed another inmate's sexual victimization during his current incarceration. He had a total score of 3.0 in child sexual victimization, and he scored 32.0 in the self-esteem scale. In a potential sexual victimization, he would prefer to disclose his experience to commutes and friends, as well as to various prison authorities.

Lastly, participants who reported both types of sexual victimization ($n = 7$) had a mean age of 30.2 years (SD8.3) and most of them were single (71.4%). Many of them were graduates of junior high school (42.8%), salaried prior to incarceration (42.8%), or unemployed (28.8%), and most of them were heterosexual (42.8%), followed by homosexual and bisexual (28.8% each). Many of them were currently sentenced for five to 20 years (71.4%), many of them were convicted for robbery (42.8%), and most of them had a past conviction for the same offences (42.8%). All of them had witnessed another inmate's sexual victimization during their current incarceration. They had a total score of 3.0 (SD1.8) in child sexual victimization and their self-esteem had an average of 26.1 (SD1.0). The vast majority of them would prefer to react violently and retaliate, as well as request a transfer to another cell in response to a potential sexual victimization (71.4% each). Detailed information on the victims' profile is provided in Tables 2–5.

3.4. Comparison between the Victimized and the Non-Victimized Participants

Victims of sexual violence were younger in age and had a lower self-esteem as compared with those not victimized. The single and divorced, the graduates of senior high school followed by those of junior high school, the unemployed prior to incarceration, as well as the homosexuals and bisexuals were overrepresented among the victimized participants. On the contrary, the non-victimized participants were mostly single, followed by married, salaried, graduates of senior high school, and heterosexual (Table 2). As regards to offence-related characteristics, those convicted in the past for different offences, those currently convicted for rape, pedophilia and pornography, and those with long sentences but not life imprisonment, were overrepresented among the victimized participants as compared with the non-victimized participants who were primarily those never convicted in the past, those currently convicted for drugs, and those with sentences less than five years (Table 3). The victimized participants were further shown to mostly prefer violent reactions and revenge as a response strategy to a potential sexual victimization as compared with the non-victimized participants who reported a higher preference for a cell transfer (Table 4). Lastly, as regards to other victimization experiences, persons who reported "attempted" or "completed" anal sex during childhood, as well as those who witnessed the victimization of other inmates, reported higher levels of victimization during incarceration as compared to those who had no similar experiences (Table 5).

4. Discussion

This is the first study that looked at the experiences of sexual victimization of incarcerated men in Greece. The small sample is a serious limitation of the study that needs to be acknowledged. Comparing key sociodemographic, offence- and sentence-related characteristics between our study participants and the 10-year average performance of the total population of Greek prisoners (http://www.ministryofjustice.gr/site/en/Leadership/Greetings.aspx), there is evidence of representativeness in some aspects (e.g., ~60.0% foreigners in total vs. 80.0% foreigners excluded from our sample based on the inclusion criteria (peak in 2011 with 72.2% of foreigner detainees in the largest prison), ~23.0% of prisoners with one month to five years imprisonment vs. 30.0% in our sample, ~8.0% of prisoners with life imprisonment vs. 6.0% in our sample, 32.0% of prisoners with drug-related violations vs. 52.0% in our sample), while there seems to be over- or underrepresentation in some other aspects (e.g., ~29.0% of prisoners in pre-trial detention vs. 2.0% in our sample and 0.3% of prisoners with debt-related violations vs. 4.0% in our sample).

In view of the above, generalizability of the study findings to the general population of Greek prisoners should be made with caution since the study had a low response rate and lacked evidence on whether the respondents differed significantly from non-respondents in terms of sexual victimization or other important risk factors. For example, the low response rate among prisoners in pretrial detention needs to be taken into consideration when interpreting the study findings, as international literature identifies them as a high-risk group for sexual victimization in prisons and our findings probably underestimate their experiences. Further to this consideration, it is worth mentioning that population-based studies (e.g., BJS, NIS-3, and SHAAP) [19] tend to report low prevalence rates (between 3% and 10%), while studies with small sample sizes or non-random sampling designs tend to report much higher prevalence figures (>25%) [12]. Most importantly, research employing expansive definitions of sexual misconduct reveal much higher prevalence rates as compared with those focusing on completed rape. Given these methodological considerations, we should identify the possibility of overestimated figures among our study findings.

Despite this limitation, this study has attempted to begin to fill the gap in our understanding of sexual abuse within prison facilities, which is considered to be a field where data and information is still scarce worldwide, due to the limited access in prison facilities [14,19]. Therefore, very little research has focused on prisoners [35,36]. What is evident from this very initial assessment of the problem is the fact that sexual assault is a problem for inmates in Greek prisons.

What seems important in the results is the fact that approximately one quarter of the inmates (26.0%) in our study were sexually assaulted by another inmate. This is consistent with previous research in male inmates in U.S., which indicated that 21% to 22% of prisoners had been subjected to sexual pressure or assault at least once [14,37]. It is, however, expected that this percentage underestimates the problem as sexual assault in prison facilities is underreported [35,38–40]. In general, the phenomenon has been said to be on the rise over the last few decades due to three major interrelated factors which include: (a) the distinct manifestations of the prison social order; (b) the correction officers' role in policing; and (c) the overcrowding [41]. These factors may be better understood with the assistance of the deprivation model, which suggests that aggressive behavior among inmates is triggered by the painful experiences inside the prisons [42].

Although our study did not generate evidence on the contribution of contextual factors in sexual misconduct, there are several institutional aspects in our study setting, which could assist us in the interpretation of our findings regarding sexual misconduct. More specifically, this particular prison facility has been shown in various CPT and Ombudsman reports to accommodate four, or even five inmates in 9.5 m^2 cells, resulting in less than 2 m^2 space available for each individual prisoner, and sometimes with one prisoner of the five sleeping on the floor [43]. In fact, overcrowding and chronic shortage of staff seems to persist in the Greek prison system, as shown in the latest CPT report (March 2016; https://rm.coe.int/168069667e). In addition to the above, the staff has been criticized for spending little time in the accommodation areas leaving prisoners unprotected. As a result, prisoners have been shown to have no trust in the management to resolve questions of intimidation and violence (CPT Report March 2016, https://rm.coe.int/168069667e).

Apart from the deprivation model, this study offers a lot of insight into potential links to the importation model, which argues that prison violence is performed by individuals, who were dysfunctional prior to incarceration [44,45]. What becomes clear from the results of this study, which may find support in the importation model, is the fact that the inmates who experienced sexual victimization seem to have certain individual characteristics that may render them vulnerable to sexual victimization in prison. For example, although the small sample size in this study did not allow us to carry out a more rigorous statistical analysis, the unemployed were shown to experience sexual victimization at a higher level than other inmates. This is not surprising under the perspective of the deprivation model, as prior unemployment is probably one aspect of an overall vulnerable profile, linked with poverty and social exclusion. This could imply that an individual leading such a profile before incarceration is considered to be vulnerable in different social contexts [44].

Likewise, the results of this study indicated that participants with a homosexual or bisexual sexual orientation experienced more sexual approaches or assaults from those reporting a heterosexual sexual orientation. In line with our finding, previous research has shown a link between sexual victimization during incarceration and sexual orientation [17,19,30,41,46]. It has been suggested that "straight" males sexually assault individuals with a non-heterosexual orientation because they consider them to be subordinate and they expect them to be submissive [47]. Likewise, in BJS surveys 2011 to 2012, non-heterosexual inmates were among the most vulnerable for sexual victimization. In 2008, the first U.S. National Former Prisoner Survey (NFPS) found 34% of bisexual males, and 39.0% of homosexual or gay males to have been sexually victimized by an inmate as compared to 3.5% of heterosexual males [17]. In line with this, the Special Rapporteur on Torture to the Human Rights Council identified this high vulnerability of non-heterosexual inmates many years ago [48] with transgender persons, especially male-to-female transgender inmates, considered to be at great risk in male prisons. However, it should be noted, that heterosexual men are less likely to report victimization due to feelings of shame, and therefore possibly resulting in the overestimation of the phenomenon among non-heterosexual men [19].

Interestingly, the victimized participants in this study were shown to have past convictions for the same or different offences than those related to their current incarceration, and long duration of sentences. Nevertheless, research has consistently shown that first-time offenders are more often the targets of sexual assaults due to being unaccustomed to the prison subculture, and therefore more vulnerable to intimidation [49,50]. The first population survey in Australia prisoners generated evidence in support of our findings, suggesting that sexual victimization is more likely to occur among first time offenders and those who had been in prison for a period exceeding five years than among other groups [19], however, this needs to be examined together with the information on the current offence. In particular, this study indicated that those who were currently convicted for robbery and drugs were overrepresented among the victimized participants. On the basis of the importation model, it is interesting to find that most of the victimized prisoners are serving time for nonviolent offences, but to survive behind bars, they are forced to adapt to the culture of brutality [44,45].

Not surprisingly, our study identified that sexual abuse in childhood was a characteristic more evident among the participants that were victimized as compared to those who were not. This is another common measure of the importation model, examined very often as part of the history of violence to assist in the estimation of risk scores [44]. Its contribution as a risk factor to the interpretation of sexual victimization has been clearly demonstrated in recent literature [18]. This could probably be attributed to problematic adaptive emotion regulation abilities, which decrease individuals' recognition of impending danger or make their vulnerability more visible to perpetrators. Past research has also found two to five times increased likelihood of victimization among those who had similar experiences prior to age 18 as compared with their counterparts [51]. The multiple victimization could potentially explain the levels of self-esteem, which were found to be lower in the victimized participants as compared with the non-victimized ones. Low self-esteem has long been shown as a major psychological aftermath for sexual violence victims, which has often been considered to be a manifestation of underlying anger [52].

What is thought to be more alarming in this study, is the fact that all the inmates who were sexually victimized reported witnessing other inmates' sexual coercion. In fact, this may imply that sexual misconduct is well-known but underreported. It has been noted that it is common for inmates to avoid reporting witnessing the victimization of others out of fear of violating the convict law, fear of being the targets of retaliation, or even fear of involving correctional officers in prisoners' matters [53–55]. Past research found 25.0% of victimized prisoners avoid reporting their victimization as they believed it would make no difference and 20.0% did the same out of fear of retaliation [56]. Other research has offered support for this finding [34]. Interestingly, while prisoners seem to support the idea of reporting such experiences, very few are likely to report their own victimization [56]. Male rape myths have been thought to highly contribute to underreporting of male sexual victimization, since they suggest that only gay men become victims due to being unable to defend themselves like "real men" do. The stigma attached to prison rape, the feelings of shame and the humiliating reporting process are some more reasons explaining why some prisoners remain quiet [57–59]. Low literacy level and education has also been noted as a factor impeding reporting and resulting in victims' low understanding of prison policies and legal procedures [60]. Interestingly, from our study, it becomes apparent that tools currently available in Greek prisons are not employed by the target group. More precisely, the Office of the Secretary General for Counter-Criminal Policy in Greece operates a hotline for complaints by inmates regarding their detention conditions, and offers a standardized "Information Booklet for the prisoners' rights" (Form A-33) together with a complaints form called "Complaints filed by detainees"(D-34), in a language that inmates understand, to file a complaint on any poor detention conditions, abuse, ill-treatment or other violations of rights and address it to any Authority they wish. Further to this, a senior Police Officer has been appointed by the General Police Directors to control and supervise the services involved in these matters (http://www.cpt.coe.int/documents/grc/2014-27-inf-eng.pdf). Despite these efforts made by the Greek Ministry of Justice, sexual violence among inmates is still a prevalent and greatly underreported problem in Greek prisons.

Further to the aforementioned, the evidence on the preferred response strategies, which was produced from this study is in line with the existing literature. More precisely, the victimized participants in our study reported that they would mostly prefer a violent reaction as a response to sexual victimization, which was not the case for the non-victimized participants, who preferred a more indirect way to respond. This probably derives from the experience of victimization and their need to retaliate. In support of this, it has been suggested that this is part of the victims' effort to prove that they can manage their own matters like "real" men. Physical retaliation could be seen also as a masculine response aimed to make it clear to others that they are not sexually interested in other men [9].

Another issue of outmost importance, is the fact that participants who experienced both types of sexual victimization (penetrative and non-penetrative) have been shown in this study to have worse performance both in child sexual victimization and self-esteem scores, as compared with those who experienced only non-penetrative victimization and those who were not victimized at all. Many of them were also found to have low educational level, shorter sentences (10 days to five years) primarily for non-violent offences, and no past convictions, which may all be indicative of an increased vulnerability. Nevertheless, we should note that despite the fact that most of the information retrieved through the current study is in line with the existing literature on the subject, it cannot be expected to provide reliable estimations on the actual size of the problem, especially among the subcategories of the victimized participants, which were underrepresented.

4.1. Current Challenges and Future Perspectives in Addressing Sexual Violence within Prison

On the basis of the results of our study, we urgently recommend to the Greek Authorities to consider this public health issue. Certain measures and interventions could be undertaken to protect those who seem to be at risk, as well as treat those who have been affected. More precisely, our study suggests that inmates with maltreatment histories in childhood, as well as inmates with lower self-esteem, are more vulnerable to sexual victimization. This evidence could be translated into certain interventions. For example, incorporating questions regarding maltreatment histories within the initial assessment of prisoners' mental health status could potentially serve as a process of early identification of signs of vulnerability that could result in higher attention paid to individuals at risk by the prison social and mental health care staff. Assessing the level of prisoners' self-esteem and designing certain individual or group interventions to improve feelings of low self-worth, could also constitute an effective measure towards the prevention of sexual victimization and re-victimization.

Our study further suggests that LGBT inmates are more vulnerable to sexual assaults. It seems, thus, important to undertake measures in the sphere of prison life to protect them, including but not limited to housing arrangements, individual showering, etc. Most importantly, it seems urgent to tackle the discrimination and stigma that LGBT people face in prison and undertake action to promote respectful relationships among prisoners, as well as improve the staff's cultural competency at correctional settings across Greece.

Our study also suggests that sexual assaults in prison are highly visible, although not disclosed. In fact, a large number of prisoners in the current study reported witnessing the victimization of other inmates, which implies that peers probably know but prefer to keep silent. Further to the aforementioned, our study indicates that victimized inmates prefer violent reactions as a means of retaliation and this in turn implies that sexual assaults may generate follow-up violent acts. It seems, thus, important both for the victims of sexual assault and for their peers, to be given multiple avenues to make confidential complaints, which should be thoroughly investigated, and the results fully communicated to complainants. Educating prisoners on formal reporting pathways, offering opportunities to report acts of retaliation, as well as providing access to advocates outside the prison system would be effective interventions in facilitating disclosure. Interventions could also target peers, friends, and family members of those who are incarcerated, who may be aware of the problem.

Future policy in Greece should aim at transforming Greek correctional settings into trauma-informed settings by setting practice standards for the prevention and early intervention to trauma among the population of prisoners, including the "Do no harm" approach, strategies for the minimization of re-traumatization, predictable and consistent limits, and staff training in responding to trauma/trauma symptoms [61,62]. Improving interpersonal functioning through effective interventions on emotion regulation would help inmates regulate negative mood states and avoid maladaptive strategies (e.g., alcohol). Individual or group cognitive behavioral therapy should be considered because it has been widely identified as the best practice for treating post-traumatic stress in trauma survivors. Future policy in Greece should also consider good practice and lessons learned from implementation of relevant policies within the correctional system of other countries. The Skills Training in Affective & Interpersonal Regulation program (STAIR) [63], is an emotion-focused treatment program for survivors of sexual abuse [64]. The "Trauma Affect Regulation: Guide for Education and Treatment" (TARGET) and the "Seeking Safety" have been developed to assist victimized individuals to understand trauma and control their emotional response [63]. Prison Rape Elimination Act (PREA) is also an ambitious piece of legislation, which could offer much to Greek policymakers, despite the conflicting evaluation outcomes and the severe criticism for low enforcement in the USA [65]. In fact, PREA aimed to sanction prison sexual violence through introducing a set of tools (e.g., technical assistance, grants, and standards). Within the PREA framework [66,67], all states in the U.S. undertook various tasks such as training of the staff and offenders, improvement or development of investigative structures, development of data collection capacities, enhancement of security by installing cameras, and development of housing options for victims. Other well-established initiatives in Europe could also provide useful insight into effective prison violence prevention, including situational measures (e.g., improved supervision) offender programs (e.g., therapeutic communities and education programs), and other "social prevention" programs [10].

4.2. Study Limitations

This study had limitations that should be acknowledged. One limitation is related to the small sample size, which precluded us from conducting more sophisticated statistical analyses that could have further aided in our understanding of the characteristics of male victims. Furthermore, the prevalence of sexual victimization estimated in our study seems to be similar with the ones reported in other studies, however, questions remain on whether we have captured the actual size of the problem.

Our sample did not include immigrants, who represent a great part of the population of inmates and whose human rights are thought to be highly violated. In fact, according to the Hellenic League of Human Rights report, there have been cases of foreign detainees with low awareness of their rights, and therefore have limited access to interpretation services and legal assistance. This highlights the need to consider the additional vulnerabilities that may be affecting those excluded from this study in order to assure that their health and human rights are protected too, especially in terms of sexual victimization. However, carrying out research with this population requires large-scale study design and a culturally sensitive approach.

Furthermore, our sample was derived from one male prison facility, and thus the results cannot be generalized or assumed to be representative of the total population of male inmates. Moreover, a high number of inmates declined to participate in the study, which may be an important confound, as we do not know how the inmates who chose not to take part in the study differed in their experiences from those who did participate. Although reminders were sent by the research team at monthly intervals, the response rate only slightly increased. There is a possibility that inmates were not convinced by the guarantees of confidentiality and this may have influenced the response rate. However, this is not surprising since high refusal rates have been reported in most studies of inmates.

Last but not least, we need to acknowledge the fact that this study used a narrow definition of sexual misconduct and relied on participants' understanding of two single questions regarding sexual victimization. It would have been more effective to introduce follow-up questions to be able to identify the characteristics of the victimization (e.g., type and nature), in order to avoid potentially overestimated instances of certain types of sexual misconduct.

5. Conclusions

Findings from this research offer an initial assessment of the problem in a country with limited information and clear policy implications, which could be used to guide large-scale surveys to improve life in prison facilities. Most importantly, vulnerable groups identified in this small sample of inmates could receive further attention in future studies and policy initiatives. Profiling victims is expected to be useful for inmates' and staff's education regarding sexual violence in prison. Furthermore, this study underlined the need to commence large-scale studies in order to obtain a reliable baseline of incidence data, as well as the need to include macro-level and structural factors in future investigations to better understand the causes of this highly prevalent phenomenon. In fact, there are additional individual and contextual aspects with potential links to sexual victimization, which were not captured in this study and should be addressed in future research. For example, as previous research suggests that the risk is greatest in the first 6 months of admittance to a correctional facility [68,69], the results would have been more informative, if participants were asked to indicate when their victimization occurred during the present incarceration. It would be further interesting to investigate sexual victimization among more diverse populations of prisoners and correctional institutions, as well as in female facilities. Revisiting the correctional sites and carrying out follow-up surveys is missing from research in correctional settings, although considered to be very important. Furthermore, future research needs to consider victimization from staff, which has been shown to be very prevalent in male prisons and was not captured in this study. Most importantly, the study stresses the need to introduce mechanisms to better monitor the problem in Greek prisons for the prison authorities to intervene in a timely manner. Further to that, measures taken in response to the problem, should not single out those at risk while overlooking other important parameters such as the potential institutional and social factors that might create the problem. Last but not least, given the fact of underreporting to correctional staff, policymakers should consider the active involvement of external organizations, such as community-based services and prisoner support groups, in the prevention of violence and the treatment of trauma [19].

Author Contributions: Conceptualization, M.P., M.G., and J.C.; methodology, M.P., A.T.; D.P., and J.C.; validation, M.P., A.T., and D.P.; formal analysis, M.P., A.T., D.P., and J.C.; investigation, M.P. and M.G.; data curation, M.P. and M.G.; writing—original draft preparation, M.P.; writing—review and editing, M.P., A.T., D.P., M.G., and J.C.; supervision, M.P.; project administration, M.G.

Funding: This research received no external funding.

Acknowledgments: Ethical approval for this project was granted by the Greek Ministry of Justice (reference no. 4161) and the prison council (reference No. 616).

Conflicts of Interest: The authors declare no conflict of interest.

References

1. Rights Watch Report 2001, US, Human Rights Developments. Available online: https://www.hrw.org/legacy/wr2k1/usa/index.html (accessed on 10 October 2018).
2. O'Donnell, I. Prison rape in context. *Br. J. Criminol.* **2004**, *44*, 241–255. [CrossRef]
3. Moller, L.; Stover, H.; Jurgens, R.; Gatherer, A.; Nikogosian, H. (Eds.) *Health in Prisons: A WHO Guide to the Essentials in Prison Health*; World Health Organization Press: Copenhagen, Denmark, 2007.
4. Stevens, A. *Coercive Sex in Prison*; Howard League for Penal Reform Press: London, UK, 2014.
5. Kunzel, R. *Criminal Intimacy: Prison and the Uneven History of Modern American Sexuality*; University of Chicago Press: Chicago, IL, USA; London, UK, 2008.

6. Wooden, W.S.; Parker, J. *Men Behind Bars: Sexual Exploitation in Prison*; Plenum Press: New York, NY, USA, 1982.
7. Connell, R.W. *Masculinities*, 2nd ed.; University of California Press: Berkeley, CA, USA, 2005.
8. Groth, A.N.; Burgess, A.W. Male rape: Offenders and victims. *Am. J. Psychiatry* **1980**, *137*, 806–810. [CrossRef] [PubMed]
9. Javaid, A. Male Rape in Law and the Courtroom. Available online: http://webjcli.org/article/view/340/434 (accessed on 3 September 2018).
10. Homel, R.; Thomson, C. Corrections Criminology. In *Causes and Prevention of Violence in Prisons*; O'Toole, S., Eyland, S., Eds.; Hawkins Press: Sydney, Australia, 2005; pp. 101–108.
11. Bottoms, A.E. *Interpersonal Violence and Social Order in Prisons*; Tonry, M., Petersilia, J., Eds.; The University of Chicago Press: Chicago, IL, USA, 1999; pp. 205–228.
12. Heilpern, D.M. *Fear or Favour: Sexual Assault of Young Prisoners*; Southern Cross University Press: Lismore, Australia, 1998.
13. Stemple, L. Male Rape and Human Rights. *Hastings Law J.* **2009**, *60*, 605–609.
14. Struckman-Johnson, C.; Struckman-Johnson, D.; Rucker, L.; Bumby, K.; Donaldson, S. Sexual coercion reported by men and women in prison. *J. Sex Res.* **1996**, *33*, 67–76. [CrossRef]
15. Beck, A.J.; Harrison, P.M. U.S. Dep't of Justice, Publ'n No. NCJ 221946, Sexual Victimization in State and Federal Prisons Reported by Inmates. 2007. Available online: http://www.ojp.usdoj.gov/bjs/pub/pdf/svljri07.pdf (accessed on 3 September 2018).
16. Beck, J.A.; Berzofsky, M.; Caspar, R.; Krebs, C. *RTI International May 2013*; NCJ 241399; U.S. Department of Justice, Office of Justice Programs, Bureau of Justice Statistics: Washington, DC, USA, 2013.
17. Beck, J.A.; Johnson, C. *Publication Sexual Victimization Reported by Former State Prisoners, 2008*; NCJ 237363; Part of the PREA Publications Series; U.S. Department of Justice, Office of Justice Programs, Bureau of Justice Statistics: Washington, DC, USA, 2012.
18. Caravaca-Sánchez, F.; Wolff, N. Understanding Polyvictimization in Prison: Prevalence and Predictors among Men Inmates in Spain. Available online: https://journals.sagepub.com/doi/abs/10.1177/0886260518775751?journalCode=jiva (accessed on 3 September 2019).
19. Simpson, P.L.; Reekie, J.; Butler, T.G.; Richters, J.; Yap, L.; Grant, L.; Richards, A.; Donovan, B. Factors Associated With Sexual Coercion in a Representative Sample of Men in Australian Prisons. *Arch Sex Behav.* **2016**, *45*, 1195–1205. [CrossRef]
20. Ahlin, E.M.; Hummer, D. Sexual victimization of juveniles incarcerated in jails and prisons: An exploratory study of prevalence and risk factors human. *Vict. Offenders* **2019**, *14*, 793–810. [CrossRef]
21. Optional protocol to the Convention against Torture and Other Cruel, Inhuman or degrading Treatment or punishment ("OpCaT"), G.a. Res. 57/199, U.n. doc. a/ReS/57/199 (Dec. 18, 2002). Available online: https://www.ohchr.org/EN/ProfessionalInterest/Pages/OPCAT.aspx (accessed on 1 February 2019).
22. International Covenant on Civil and political Rights, adopted dec. 16, 1966, 999 U.n.T.S. 171 (entered into force March 23, 1976). Available online: https://treaties.un.org/doc/publication/unts/volume%20999/volume-999-i-14668-english.pdf (accessed on 1 February 2019).
23. Giotakos, O.; Markianos, M.; Vaidakis, N.; Christodoulou, G.N. Aggression, impulsivity, plasma sex hormones, and biogenic amine turnover in a forensic population of rapists. *J. Sex. Marital Ther.* **2003**, *29*, 215–225. [CrossRef]
24. Giotakos, O.; Markianos, M.; Vaidakis, N.; Christodoulou, G.N. Sex hormones and biogenic amine turnover of sex offenders in relation to their temperament and character dimensions. *Psychiatry Res.* **2004**, *127*, 185–193. [CrossRef]
25. Council of Europe. Annual Penal Statistics, SPACE I, Survey 2011. Strasbourg 3 May 2013, PC-CP\space\documents\PC-CP(2013)5. Available online: http://www3.unil.ch/wpmu/space/files/2014/04/SPACE1_2011_English.pdf (accessed on 21 April 2018).
26. Amnesty International. Amnesty International Annual Report 2013—Greece, 23 May 2013. Available online: http://www.refworld.org/docid/519f519b4b.html (accessed on 21 April 2018).
27. Council of Europe's Committee for the Prevention of Torture and Inhuman or Degrading Treatment or Punishment, Report 2012. Available online: http://www.cpt.coe.int/documents/grc/2012-01-inf-eng.pdf (accessed on 1 February 2019).

28. Council of Europe's Committee for the Prevention of Torture and Inhuman or Degrading Treatment or Punishment, Report 2013. Available online: http://www.cpt.coe.int/documents/grc/2014-10-16-eng.htm (accessed on 1 February 2019).
29. Struckman-Johnson, C.; Struckman-Johnson, D. A comparison of sexual coercion experiences reported by men and women in prison. *J. Interpers. Violence* **2006**, *21*, 1591–1615. [CrossRef]
30. Hensley, C.; Koscheski, M.; Tewksbury, R. Examining the characteristics of male sexual assault targets in a southern maximum-security prison. *J. Interpers. Violence* **2005**, *20*, 667–679. [CrossRef]
31. Tewksbury, R. Fear of sexual assault in prison inmates. *Prison J.* **1989**, *69*, 62–71. [CrossRef]
32. Rosenberg, M. *Society and the Adolescent Self-Image*; Princeton University Press: Princeton, NJ, USA, 1965.
33. Koumi, I.; Tsiantis, J. Smoking trends in adolescence: Report on a Greek school-based peer-led intervention aimed at prevention. *Health Promot. Int.* **2001**, *16*, 65–72. [CrossRef] [PubMed]
34. Papadakaki, M.; Tzamalouka, G.S.; Chatzifotiou, S.; Chliaoutakis, J. Seeking for risk factors of Intimate Partner Violence (IPV) in a Greek national sample: The role of self-esteem. *J. Interpers. Violence* **2009**, *24*, 732–750. [CrossRef] [PubMed]
35. Richters, J.; Butler, T.; Schneider, K.; Yap, L.; Kirkwood, K.; Grant, L.; Richards, A.; Smith, A.M.; Donovan, B. Consensual sex between men and sexual violence in Australian prisons. *Arch. Sex. Behav.* **2012**, *41*, 517–524. [CrossRef]
36. Wolff, N.; Shi, J. Patterns of victimization and feelings of safety inside prison: The experience of male and female inmates. *Crime Delinq.* **2011**, *57*, 29–55. [CrossRef]
37. Struckman-Johnson, C.; Struckman-Johnson, D. Sexual coercion rates in seven midwestern prison facilities for men. *Prison J.* **2000**, *80*, 379–390. [CrossRef]
38. Gear, S. Behind the Bars of Masculinity: Male Rape and Homophobia in and About South African Men's Prisons. *Sexualities* **2007**, *10*, 209–216. [CrossRef]
39. Robertson, J.E. A clean heart and an empty head: The Supreme Court and sexual terrorism in prison. *North Carol Law Rev.* **2003**, *81*, 434–482.
40. Felson, R.B.; Cundiff, P.; Painter-Davis, N. Age and sexual assault in correctional facilities: A blocked opportunity approach. *Criminology* **2012**, *50*, 887–911. [CrossRef]
41. Lara, A. Forced integration of gay, bisexual and transgendered inmates in California state prisons: From protected minority to exposed victims. *South Calif. Interdiscip. Law J.* **2010**, *19*, 589–594.
42. Innes, C.A. Patterns of misconduct in the federal prison system. *Crim. Justice Rev.* **1997**, *22*, 157–174. [CrossRef]
43. Koulouris, N.K.; Aloskofis, W. *Prison Conditions in Greece*; European Prison Observatory Press: Rome, Italy, 2013.
44. Berg, M.T.; DeLisi, M. The correctional melting pot: Race, ethnicity, citizenship, and prison violence. *J. Crim. Justice* **2006**, *34*, 631–642. [CrossRef]
45. Gover, A.R.; MacKenzie, D.L.; Armstrong, G. Importation and deprivation explanations of juveniles' adjustment to correctional facilities. *Int. J. Offender Ther. Comp. Criminol.* **2000**, *44*, 450–467. [CrossRef]
46. Broadus, K. The Criminal Justice System and Trans People. *Temple Political & Civil Rights Low Rev.* **2009**, *561*, 569–575.
47. *National Prison Rape Elimination Report*; NPREC Press: Washington, DC, USA, 2011. Available online: https://www.ncjrs.gov/pdffiles1/226680.pdf (accessed on 3 February 2019).
48. Special Rapporteur on Torture to the Human Rights Council, UN. 2001. Available online: https://www.ohchr.org/Documents/Issues/Discrimination/A.HRC.19.41_English.pdf (accessed on 3 February 2019).
49. Gear, S.; Ngubeni, K. *Daai Ding: Sex, Sexual Violence and Coercion in Men's Prisons*; Centre for the Study of Violence and Reconciliation Press: Johannesburg, South Africa, 2002.
50. Gear, S. *Fear, Violence and Sexual Violence in a Gauteng Juvenile Correctional Centre for Males*; Briefing Report No 2; Centre for the Study of Violence and Reconciliation Press: Johannesburg, South Africa, 2007.
51. Wolff, N.; Shi, J.; Blitz, C.; Siegel, J. Understanding sexual victimization inside prisons: Factors that predict risk. *Criminol. Public Policy* **2007**, *6*, 201–231. [CrossRef]
52. Anderson, C.L. Males as Sexual Assault Victims. *J. Homosex.* **1982**, *7*, 2–3. [CrossRef]
53. Banbury, S. Coercive sexual behavior in British prisons as reported by adult ex-prisoners. *Howard J. Crim. Justice* **2004**, *43*, 2–113. [CrossRef]

54. Alarid, L.F. Sexual perspectives of incarcerated bisexual and gay men: The county jail protective custody experience. *Prison J.* **2000**, *80*, 1–80. [CrossRef]
55. Beck, A.J.; Hughes, T. *Sexual Violence Reported by Correctional Authorities, 2004*; NCJ-210333; U.S. Department of Justice, Bureau of Justice Statistics Press: Washington, DC, USA, 2005.
56. Byrne, J.M.; Hummer, D. Myths and realities of prison violence: A review of the evidence. *Vict. Offender* **2007**, *2*, 77–90. [CrossRef]
57. Fowler, K.S.; Blackburn, G.A.; Marquart, W.J.; Mulling, L.J. Inmates cultural beliefs about sexual violence and their relationship to definitions of sexual assault. *J. Offender Rehabil.* **2010**, *49*, 180–190. [CrossRef]
58. Rumney, P.N. Policing male rape and sexual assault. *J. Crim. Law* **2008**, *72*, 67–86. [CrossRef]
59. Robertson, J. "Turning-Out" of boys in a man's prison: Why and how we need to amend the prison rape elimination act. *Indiana Law Rev.* **2010**, *44*, 819–852.
60. Kubiak, S.P.; Brenner, H.; Bybee, D.; Campbell, R.; Fedock, G. Reporting Sexual Victimization During Incarceration: Using Ecological Theory as a Framework to Inform and Guide Future Research. *Trauma Violence Abus.* **2018**, *19*, 94–106. [CrossRef] [PubMed]
61. Giavrimis, P. The Training of Prison Guards: The Case of Greece. *IJCST* **2012**, *5*, 871–885.
62. Benedict, A. *Using Trauma-Informed Practices to Enhance Safety and Security in Women's Correctional Facilities*; National Resource Center on Justice Involved Women Press: Cincinnati, OH, USA, 2010.
63. Cloitre, M.; Koenen, K.; Cohen, L.; Han, H. Skills training plus exposure therapy may reduce post traumatic stress in women who experienced childhood sexual abuse. *J. Consult. Clin. Psychol.* **2002**, *70*, 1067–1074. [CrossRef]
64. Miller, N.A.; Najavits, L.M. Creating trauma-informed correctional care: A balance of goals and environment. *Eur. J. Psychotramatol.* **2012**, *3*, 17246. [CrossRef]
65. Substance Abuse and Mental Health Services Administration. *Treatment Improvement Protocol*; Series 57; Trauma-Informed Care in Behavioral Health Services (TIP): Rockville, MD, USA, 2014.
66. Eggert, E. Violence and Silence: The Prison Rape Elimination Act and Beyond. *Tapestries Interwoven Voices Local Glob. Identities* **2018**, *7*, 6. Available online: http://digitalcommons.macalester.edu/tapestries/vol7/iss1/6 (accessed on 1 February 2019).
67. *Bureau of Justice Statistics Status Report: Data Collections for the Prison Rape Elimination Act of 2003*; Bureau of Justice Statistics Press: Washington, DC, USA, 2004.
68. Struckman-Johnson, C.; Struckman-Johnson, D. Stopping prison rape: The evolution of standards recommended by PREA's National Prison Rape Elimination Commission. *Prison J.* **2013**, *93*, 335–354. [CrossRef]
69. Hensley, C.; Castle, T.; Tewksbury, R. Inmate-to-inmate sexual coercion in a prison for women. *J. Offender Rehabil.* **2003**, *37*, 77–87. [CrossRef]

© 2019 by the authors. Licensee MDPI, Basel, Switzerland. This article is an open access article distributed under the terms and conditions of the Creative Commons Attribution (CC BY) license (http://creativecommons.org/licenses/by/4.0/).

Article

Testing the Utility of the Neural Network Model to Predict History of Arrest among Intimate Partner Violent Men

Julia C. Babcock [1,*] and Jason Cooper [2]

1. Department of Psychology, University of Houston, 4800 Calhoun Rd, Houston, TX 77004, USA
2. Private Practice, Plano, TX 75074, USA; JasonCooper623@gmail.com
* Correspondence: jbabcock@uh.edu; Tel.: +1-713-743-8621

Received: 28 September 2018; Accepted: 28 December 2018; Published: 10 January 2019

Abstract: Risk assessments are typically based on retrospective reports of factors known to be correlated with violence recidivism in simple linear models. Generally, these linear models use only the perpetrators' reports. Using a community sample of couples recruited for recent male-to-female intimate partner violence (IPV; $N = 97$ couples), the current study compared non-linear neural network models to traditional linear models in predicting a history of arrest in men who perpetrate IPV. The neural network models were found to be superior to the linear models in their predictive power. Models were slightly improved by adding victims' report. These findings suggest that the prediction of violence arrest be enhanced through the use of neural network models and by including collateral reports.

Keywords: intimate partner violence; neural network; violence risk assessment

1. Introduction

Psychologists and legal experts regularly make use of tools designed to predict criminal recidivism. Although these tools have made significant improvements in recent decades, there is general agreement that experts are poor at predicting which inmates will recidivate and which will not [1]. One reason why current methods for predicting recidivism perform poorly is that they treat all inmates as a homogenous group without considering type of crime or motivation for the criminal act [2]. Early research suggested that measures focusing on specific types of criminals using criminogenic theories may possess greater predictive power than models lacking in specificity [3]. Therefore, tools are needed that are designed to predict a specific type of violence recidivism in specific subpopulations of criminals, such as perpetrators of intimate partner violence (IPV).

Secondly, researchers generally use linear models such as logistic regression to predict recidivism. However, linear models are limited in their ability to predict complex phenomena such as recidivism [4]. For example, linear models assume that the independent variables are normally distributed and are not correlated although most psychosocial measures are correlated. Neural Networks (NN) are non-linear models that do not have some of the limiting properties of linear models. For example, they do not require that independent variables be uncorrelated, or normally distributed [5]. Thus, NN may have a greater ability than linear models to predict which men are likely to commit IPV in the future and which are not.

Third, models of recidivism have not typically taken both perpetrator and victim report into account. Although IPV has been shown to be better predicted by perpetrator characteristics than victim's characteristics, the addition of the victim's report of the perpetrators characteristics and history may enhance the model's predictive power over models that rely on the report of only the victim or only the perpetrator.

1.1. Risk Assessment for Intimate Partner Violence

IPV is a complex and intractable public health problem that affects many people around the world [6]. It includes physical (e.g., grabbing, choking, punching), psychological (e.g., yelling, put-downs), and sexual (e.g., rape, coercion for sexual acts) abuse towards a former or current romantic partner [7]. Generally, IPV has been thought to be motivated by men's need for power and control over their female partner [8]. In the United States, an average of 20 people per minute are victims of physical violence by a romantic partner, resulting in over ten million male and female victims within a given year [7]. According to the most recent national survey, nearly one in four women (22.3%) and one in seven men (14%) have been victims of severe physical violence by a romantic partner in their lifetime [9]. Homicide is one of the leading causes of death for women under the age of 44 with 3519 women murdered in the United States in 2015 [10]. In a review of femicides over the past decade, 55.3% were murdered by their intimate partners [10].

Among prison inmates, nearly one quarter (22%) have been convicted of family violence [11]. About 90% of offenders in state prisons for family violence had at a minimum caused physical injury to their victim and a staggering 28% of those offenders had murdered their partner [11]. Although recidivism rates are high for a wide variety of crimes, they are particularly high in cases of IPV [12]. Even after arrest and court-mandated interventions, between 15% and 60% of IPV perpetrators reassualt within three years [13–17]. Given the risk of serious injury and death that partners of violent men and women face, it is particularly important that we are able to distinguish those individuals who will be arrested and are repeat offenders of IPV. However, most researchers use linear methods to predict recidivism which have false positive and false negative rates that exceed 50%. New methods of predicting recidivism are not likely to improve the accuracy of the predictions without developing theories and tools upon which to build and assess predictive models [4].

1.2. IPV Risk Assessment Tools

With the recent advances in our understanding of IPV and its related factors, there has been a proliferation of measures designed to assess for the likelihood and severity of future incidents of IPV, including the Spouse Abuse Risk Assessment (SARA) [18]), the Domestic Violence Screening Instrument (DVSI) [19]), the Ontario Domestic Assault Risk Assessment (ODARA) [20]) and the Domestic Violence Risk Appraisal Guide (DVRAG) [21] The present study utilizes two commonly used measures of IPV risk factors; the Personal and Relationships Profile (PRP) [22], completed by the male perpetrator and the Danger Assessment Scale (DA) [23], completed by the female victim.

1.3. Neural Networks

Such risk assessment tools are generally entered into multiple regression models to predict arrest. Supervised NN models are similar to multiple regression models with the exception that they use a new class of nonlinear forms [24,25]. A NN is a mathematical simulation of a collection of idealized "neurons" and how they are connected. These models have a set of input neurons and a set of output neurons and which are not analyzed independently, but rather in the context of all variables entered with it to be processed as a whole [26]. One of the greatest strengths of NNs is their ability to adapt. Once the network designer sets up the basic parameters of the model, the model will examine the input and give a certain output. That output is then compared to the correct outcome and if the actual outcome does not match the desired output the model makes small adjustments to the connections between the neurons and tries again with the next piece of input. As this process is repeated, the model becomes increasingly adept at predicting the correct output based on the specific input it is given [5].

NNs are more flexible and may be better suited than multiple regression for the non-linear relationships often found in complex, real-world applications. For example, Pao [27] found that NNs were better able than regression models to predict debt ratio and identify important determinants of capital structure among various industries in Taiwan. Barcelos-Tronto, da Silva, and Sant'Anna [28] found that NNs outperformed linear models in predicting the amount of resources a manager would need to allocate to a particular project. In medical settings, NN models generally outperform their linear counterpart in predicting mortality and disease-free survival [29], although not always [30,31]. A meta-analysis of medical research suggests that NNs generally outperform regression models [32], especially in smaller samples ($N < 5000$).

NNs are particularly adept at identifying the kinds of adaptive and nonlinear systems found in biology and the social sciences [4], although they are more commonly used today in real estate appraisal, stock price prediction, and voice and image recognition software [33]. One study applying NN to emergency room data to identify victims of domestic violence [26] found that it could predict group membership with 78% sensitivity and 89% specificity. However, this study did not compare the accuracy of NN vs. linear models or examine the area under the curve (AUC), a standard measure of accuracy. Another predicting hospital violence found that the NN models were superior to linear regressions in terms of sensitivity, specificity and AUC [34]. Other researchers using both types of models to predict recidivism among offenders released from prisons [4] or psychiatric hospitals [35] found no improvement in NN models over and above linear models in predicting recidivism. However, in a larger study of offenders released from prison, Palocsay and colleagues [36] found that NNs were superior to multivariate logistic regressions in predicting overall recidivism. Thus, the research on the advantages of NN when applied to criminal justice data is mixed. No study to date has applied NN modeling to perpetrators of domestic violence.

1.4. The Current Study

The current study tested four models designed to identify perpetrators with a history of arrest. One linear model included only data collected from the perpetrator of IPV, while a second linear model added information collected from the partner of the perpetrator. Similarly, two supervised NNs were created, one lacking data from the partner and the other will include the partner's data. To use the perpetrator-only model as an illustration, the NN will be given information on each of the relevant variables for a particular male. The model will rate the importance of each variable, guessing, for example, that a history of substance abuse is more important than a history of childhood abuse. The model will then guess as to whether that particular male has a history of arrest or not. If the model is correct then no adjustments will be made to the model. However, if the model is incorrect regarding his arrest history then minor changes will be made such as increasing the importance of violent history or reducing the importance of a history of childhood abuse. The model's ability to accurately predict which men have a history of incarceration and which do not will then be measured via several comparison criteria discussed below. It is hypothesized that the NN models will be better able to predict history of arrest in perpetrators of IPV than linear models and that models that include victim report will outperform those that lack victim report.

2. Materials and Methods

2.1. Participants

Adult, heterosexual cohabitating couples with a history of IPV were recruited for this study through newspaper advertisements recruiting "couples experiencing conflict". To meet inclusion criteria, women must have reported two or more male-to-female acts of physical violence in the past year on the Conflict Tactics Scale-2 (CTS-2) [37]. To meet criteria for the distressed/nonviolent group, women must have reported no violence in the past year, no serious violence ever, and a score of 5 or lower on a 7-point scale of relationship satisfaction [38].

Participants were recruited from a large city in the Southern United States. The advertisement specified that couples must be 18 years of age or older, married or living together as if married for at least 6 months, and be able to read and write in English ($N = 92$ dyads). Twenty of those couples failed to adequately complete the necessary measures leaving 72 couples to be included in the analyses. The mean age of the men was 32 with a range of 19 to 52 years of age. Nearly one-third of the participants reported they were unemployed at the time of the study. The mean income was approximately $30,000 per year with the highest earner reporting annual income of $130,000. The average length of time that couples had been in their current relationship was 6 years. The racial make-up of the sample consisted of African Americans (56%), Caucasians (26%), Latino (10%), Asian (6%), and those who selected "Other" (3%). Roughly half (56%) of the males reported having children. No participants reported having abused their children or of having knowledge of children being abused.

Of the IPV men, 60% reported a history of arrest and 10% had been arrested on a domestic violence charge. Seven percent reported having been arrested on both a domestic violence charge and a charge other than domestic violence. Nearly one-third of the males had a history of incarceration in either a jail or prison. Of those with a history of incarceration, the majority had only been incarcerated once. The participant with the greatest number of incarcerations had been in prison or jail 5 times. The shortest length of incarceration was 2 weeks and the longest was 192 months with a mean of 39 months.

2.2. Procedures

Data were collected as part of a larger study of IPV [39]. Female partners were screened over the phone using the CTS-2 [37] and the Short Marital Adjustment Test [38]. Couples where the women reported at least two male-to-female physically abusive acts in the past year were screened in. During the first 3 h session, only men completed questionnaires and participated in computer-based tasks. Men were paid $30 for participation in this session. During the second 3 h session, male and female participants completed questionnaires independently, including the PRP and DA. For safety, both members of the couple were separately interviewed and independently debriefed to answer any questions and to assess their present levels of anger, the partners were reunited and paid $35 each for their participation in the second session.

2.3. Safety Measures

This study was fully approved by the University of Houston Internal Review Board, Social Sciences Committee. In order to maintain the safety of the participants, safety procedures developed by Dr. Anne Ganley were used [40]. Following the assessment, participants were placed in separate rooms and debriefed to assess danger and safety. When necessary, safety plans were developed. All participants received referrals for community resources including, but not limited to, counseling services, hotline numbers, and shelters. Female participants were telephoned one week later to determine if their participation in the research project had caused any negative events. In no cases did women report violence due to participation in the assessments.

Measures

The Personal and Relationship Profile. Straus and colleagues [22]) created the comprehensive Personal and Relationships Profile (PRP) to be administered by researchers or clinicians as a stand-alone measure to assess risk factors associated with IPV. The PRP is a 187 item, 21 scale measure designed for research on intimate partner violence and as a screening tool in clinical settings. The PRP assess for 14 personal variables (antisocial personality, borderline personality, criminal history, depression, gender hostility, neglect history, post-traumatic stress, social desirability, social integration, substance abuse, stressful conditions, sexual abuse history, violence approval and violent socialization) and eight relationship variables (anger management, conflict management, communication problems, conflict, dominance, jealousy, negative attributions, relationship commitment and relationship distress). The items are scored 1 (strongly disagree), 2 (disagree), 3 (agree), 4 (strongly agree). The 21 subscales of the PRP have strong empirical support linking them to IPV. Straus [41–43]) examined the correlation of nation-to-nation differences in scores on eight PRP scales, providing strong evidence for the PRP's concurrent validity with similar measures.

The Danger Assessment. The Danger Assessment (DA) [23] is a tool designed to assess the likelihood of serious injury or death occurring as a result of IPV. Unlike the PRP, which is completed by perpetrators, the DA is a violence risk assessment tool designed for female victims. Questions on the DA are designed to assess several risk factors associated with IPV such as the male's history of violence and incarceration, his use of violence to obtain sex, access to weapons and his history of substance abuse. The measure also assesses relationship variables such his level of jealousy and the degree to which she believes he attempts to control her daily activities. It is also a good predictor of IPV recidivism and homicide. A retrospective validation study of the DA compared cases of femicide with cases of IPV in which the female victim was not killed. This study found that 90% of the cases included fell within the receiver operator curve (ROC) suggesting that the DA is adept at identifying cases of lethal IPV in relation to non-lethal IPV [43]. Roehl et al. [44] examined data provided by 1307 battered women and compared the test results of the DA with two other risk assessment questionnaires and the victims' perception of risk. The DA had the highest correlation with subsequent abuse, although the correlation was small ($r = 0.38$).

The DA originally consisted of 15 items selected based on previous research on factors related to IPV as well as input from women in battered women's shelters. Questions are designed to assess several risk factors associated with IPV such as the male's history of violence and incarceration, his use of violence to obtain sex, access to weapons and his history of substance abuse. Other items more directly assess his level of violence by measuring whether or not his violence is increasing in severity, if he has choked his victim, his history of threats to commit suicide, and history of suicide attempts [44]. Item 14 of the DA is related to child abuse and was omitted from the DA as an endorsement of that item would mandate a report to Child Protective Services.

2.4. Comparison Criteria

When assessing the accuracy of recidivism prediction models, the most commonly used indicators are: (a) the false-positive rate (FPR) which is the proportion of non-recidivists incorrectly predicted by the model as recidivists, and (b) the false-negative rate (FNR) or the proportion of recidivists incorrectly predicted as being non-recidivists and (c) the percentage of total correct predictions (TCP) [4]. One limitation of FPR, FNR, and TCP is that these scores are influenced by the base rate of recidivists found in the sample. Thus, the FPR, FNR, and TCP do not generalize beyond the sample and are not particularly useful in cross-study comparisons of the effectiveness of prediction models [45].

In addition to the criteria employed by Caulkins and colleagues [4], Receiver Operating Characteristic (ROC) analyses were conducted. The ROC is a graphical plot of the true positive rate against the false positive rate for binary classifiers. The ROC analysis provides tools to compare various models and select those with optimal performance. A plot displays a diagonal line that marks chance classification as well as a curve marking the model's classification. Larger areas under the curve (AUC) values represent higher levels of accuracy. This analysis calculates the sensitivity and specificity of each risk factor combination as well as the chances of correctly identifying those with a history of incarceration and those without. Sensitivity refers to the likelihood a test will produce a positive result when the condition is present (true positive) and specificity refers to the likelihood that a test will produce a negative result when the condition is not present (true negative). An AUC value of 0.80 or above suggests the model has good accuracy levels [46]. Good models also typically possess a sensitivity above 80% and specificity of 60% or better.

3. Results

3.1. Data Analysis

SPSS 20 was used to construct several NN models which varied in the number of hidden layers and the number of neurons in each hidden layer. The models were created using 70 percent of the data, and their accuracy in validation was tested on the remaining 30 percent of the data. Cross validation was used to prevent over-training of the model and minimize the generalization error. By partitioning the data into subsets, analyzing one subset and comparing the results to the second subset, the model is prevented from "over-learning" the training data.

Regression models were also created and tested with SPSS 20 using the Stepwise (Backward/Wald) method. The logistic regression model analyses included Hosmer–Lemeshow goodness of fit chi-square. The models were created using a stepwise method originally entering all 23 variables used in the NN model. Only four variables met criteria for inclusion in the model using men's report only, conflict, sexual abuse history, relationship distress and substance abuse, chi-Square = 2.73 (df = 8, p = 0.950) (See Table 1). Five variables were included in the logistic regression adding women's report on the DA scale (See Table 2), Chi-Square = 4.18 (df = 8, p = 0.841). Both linear models demonstrated an improvement over the null model.

Table 1. Summary of Logistic Regression Analyses in model that did not include victim report.

Predictor	B	SE B	e^B
Conflict	0.669	0.663	1.952
Sexual Abuse History	0.946	0.599	2.575
Relationship Distress	0.196	0.593	0.822
Substance Abuse	2.210	0.618	0.110
Constant	0.926	1.569	2.523

Note: e^B = exponentiated B. * p < 0.05. ** p < 0.01. *** p < 0.001. Hosmer–Lemeshow chi-Square = 2.73 (df = 8, p = 0.950)

Table 2. Summary of Logistic Regression Analyses in model including victim report.

Predictor	B	SE B	e^B
Conflict	0.669	0.664	1.935
Sexual Abuse History	1.032	0.614	2.807
Relationship Distress	0.173	0.599	0.841
Substance Abuse	2.205	0.632	0.110
Danger Assessment	0.204	0.233	0.816
Constant	0.947	1.574	2.578

Note: e^B = exponentiated B. * p < 0.05. ** p < 0.01. *** p < 0.001. Hosmer–Lemeshow Chi-Square = 4.18 (df = 8, p = 0.841).

3.2. Performance of Models

The performance of all four models across all four criteria can be found in Table 3. Among FPR, FNR and TPC, the TPC value is most commonly reported in studies that compare classification models as it is the simplest to interpret. The TPC of the NNs is higher than the regression models, suggesting that NNs correctly classify a higher percentage of the participants than linear models. Although the FPR, FNR, and TPC are useful indicators of the model's performance, they cannot be directly compared to determine which model was most effective. The Receiver Operating Characteristic is a graph used to illustrate and evaluate the performance of a model used in binary classification. The Area Under the Curve is a value that allows for direct comparison of the models by comparing the relative ratio of sensitivity to specificity for each model. It is essentially a measure of the model's ability to classify a participant. As was hypothesized, NN models were more effective than the linear models in predicting history of arrest, and models that included victim report outperformed models that did not include victim report.

Table 3. Comparison of regression and neural network models.

Model	FPR	FRN	TPC	AUC
Neural Network Models				
Men's Data Only	19%	25%	85%	0.962
Men's + Victim Report	17%	20%	85%	0.964
Logistic Regression Models				
Men's Data Only	39%	32%	65%	0.809
Men's + Victim Report	34%	24%	69%	0.812

Note: FPR = false-positive rate; FNR = the false-negative rate; TCP = percent total correct predictions; AUC = area under the curve.

4. Discussion

When compared to linear models, the NNs were better able to predict which participants had a history of arrest, as evidenced by their superior AUC values. This suggests that non-linear models such as NNs may prove more useful in real-world settings when the goal is classification of complex phenomena. NNs may be particularly adept at predicting specific means of recidivism such as IPV as they have fewer of the limitations of linear models that were discussed earlier.

Models that included victim report outperformed models that did not include victim report, although by only a marginal amount. The current study found that the addition of a second source of information would enhance the model's predictive power. For both the linear approach and the NN approach, the models that included victim report performed slightly better than models that did not include victim report. This suggests that adding victim report data may improve the ability of judges, parole boards etc. to predict who will commit acts of domestic violence in the future and who will not. It is likely that additional sources of information, such as parole officers, family members and others who know the perpetrator, will increase our predictive ability as well. However, involving victims of crime in the criminal justice system may not warrant the increased risk to their safety [47].

Tu [48] and others continue to argue that logistic regression is the clear choice when the goal of model development is to examine causal relationship among variables. This study contributes to the growing body of evidence suggesting that NNs are superior to standard linear models. There has recently been a call to develop models that incorporate both regression and NN models because a serious limitation of NNs is their tendency to over-fit the data during the training process, which limits the model's performance during testing [28]. Regression models have less potential for over-fitting because the range of functions they can model is more limited. Therefore, hybrid models combining the linear and NN models may be preferable. For example, epidemiologists have developed models for newly diagnosed cases of liver disorders by combining the two approaches [49]. Microbiologists have combined linear and NNs to model *Escherichia coli* growth [50]. Attempts at combining the models focuses on using linear models to set parameter limits to constrain the NN and prevent over training. Future research in this area would do well to examine the strengths and weaknesses of the two approaches and design models that incorporate the best of both.

This study suggests that non-linear models that include corroborating reports, such as victims' reports, may be more useful in clinical and forensic settings. Given the serious consequences of domestic violence, any improvement in our ability to predict recidivism may save not only money in legal and correctional costs but also lives. IPV causes tremendous physical and emotional pain, thus even modest improvement in prediction garnered by the use of these models may have dramatic impact. Better models may help the justice system to identify perpetrators likely to recidivate and give them longer sentences or more intensive interventions in order to protect families.

4.1. Limitations

A limitation of this study is that it is based on retrospective reports of arrests and incarceration. Ideally, one would conduct a prospective, longitudinal study of identified batterers and predict via NN models subsequent arrest and incarceration. Hagan and King [51] note that few studies have actually developed tools for predicting recidivism and tested them via longitudinal studies on former inmates. Like many previous studies, this study used an analogue design, using history of incarceration as a proxy for future recidivism. However, recidivism and history of arrest are not synonymous but are used interchangeably in the current study.

Another significant limitation is the reliance on self- and partner-reported history of arrest and incarceration as a proxy of recidivism in this cross-sectional study. Corroborating police reports would be useful as an adjunct outcome variable. Moreover, both perpetrators and victims may underreport the frequency and severity of violence in the home. However, this study was primarily a demonstration of the utility of non-linear modeling to predict group membership rather than an attempt to model recidivism.

A community sample of cohabitating couples was recruited for the current study and these findings may not generalize to shelter samples, court-mandated or incarcerated samples. Moreover, the small was relatively small. Although small sample sizes have been found to reduce the efficacy of both types of models, there has been research conducted that demonstrates both linear and NN models are equally impacted by small samples [52]. Thus, while the relatively small sample size may have affected model fit, it did not likely impact the relative performance of the models.

4.2. Future Directions

Additional studies should be longitudinal in nature, using clearly defined criteria for measuring recidivism. Longitudinal studies would allow for an analysis of how these predictor variables change over time and would add a layer of complexity to the prediction that would be well suited for non-linear models. In an applied setting, data could be collected from individuals recently released on parole and that data could be continuously added to the model, thus increasing the predictive power of the model as it has the most recent information regarding the parolee.

There are various types of NNs that have been developed, each differing in the method by which they arrive at a final means of classifying a participant. For example, Radial basis function networks and Kohonen self-organizing networks differ from the feed-forward network used in the current study. Additional research exploring these various types of networks and their ability to discriminate between recidivists and non-recidivists may be of further use to professionals who must make decisions regarding sentencing, probation, and parole.

This study suggests that additional sources of information may make significant improvements in model performance. Thus, future studies should examine which sources of information are most useful. While gaining collateral information aids the model, the cost of obtaining such information may outweigh the benefits. This study suggests that the advantages of nonlinear NN modeling outweighs any improvement in accuracy than simply adding collateral reporting to a linear model.

Author Contributions: This research was based on a dissertation completed by J.C. to the University of Houston Department of Psychology. J.C. was responsible for conceptualization, formal analysis, and writing—original draft preparation. J.C.B. was responsible for writing—review and editing, supervision, and funding acquisition.

Funding: This research was funded by University of Houston, Small Grants.

Conflicts of Interest: The authors declare no conflict of interest. The funders had no role in the design of the study; in the collection, analyses, or interpretation of data; in the writing of the manuscript, or in the decision to publish the results.

References

1. Gottfredson, D.; Snyder, H. Statistical approaches to assessing risk. OJJDP Fact Sheet. *Psychol. Assess.* **2002**, *12*, 19–30.
2. Fagan, T.J.; Ax, R.K. *Correctional Mental Health Handbook*; Sage Publications: Thousand Oaks, CA, USA, 2003.
3. Campbell, M.A.; French, S.; Gendreau, P. The Prediction of Violence in Adult Offenders: A Meta-Analytic Comparison of Instruments and Methods of Assessment. *Crim. Justice Behav.* **2009**, *36*, 567. [CrossRef]

4. Caulkins, J.; Cohen, J.; Gorr, W.; Wei, J. Predicting Criminal Recidivism: A Comparison of Neural Network Models with Statistical Methods. *J. Crim. Justice* **1996**, *24*, 227–240. [CrossRef]
5. Principe, J.C.; Euliano, N.R.; Lefebvre, W.C. *Neural and Adapive Systems: Fundamentals through Simulations*; John Wiley & Sons: New York, NY, USA, 2000.
6. Dunford, F.W. Determining Program Success. *Crime Delinquincy* **2000**, *46*, 3.
7. Breiding, M.; Basile, K.; Smith, S.; Black, M.; Mahendra, R. *Intimate Partner Violence Surveillance: Uniform Definitions and Recommended Data Elements, Version 2*; National Center for Injury Prevention and Control, Centers for Disease Control and Prevention: Atlanta, GA, USA, 2015.
8. Pence, E.; Paymar, M. *Education Groups for Men Who Batter: The Duluth Model*; Springer: New York, NY, USA, 1993.
9. Breiding, M.; Chen, J.; Black, M. *Intimatepartner Vioelnce in the United States*; National Center for Injury Prevention and Control, Centers for Disease Control and Prevention: Atlanta, GA, USA, 2014.
10. Petrosky, E.; Blair, J.M.; Betz, C.J.; Fowler, K.A.; Jack, S.P.; Lyons, B.H. Racial and Ethnic Differences in Homicides of Adult Women and the Role of Intimate Partner Violence—United States, 2003. *Morb. Mortal. Wkly. Rep.* **2017**, *66*, 741–746. [CrossRef] [PubMed]
11. Durose, M.R.; Harlow, C.W.; Langan, P.A.; Motivans, M.; Rantala, R.R.; Smith, E.L. *Family Violence Statistics: Including Statistics on Strangers and Acquaintances*; US Department of Justice, Office of Justice Programs, Bureau of Justice Statistics: Washington, DC, USA, 2005.
12. Gondolf, E. Reassault at 30-Months after Batterer Program Intake. *Int. J. Offender Ther. Comp. Criminol.* **2000**, *44*, 111. [CrossRef]
13. Buzawa, E.; Hotaling, G.T.; Klein, A.; Byrne, J. *Response to Domestic Violence in a Pro-Active Court Setting*; University of Massachusetts: Lowell, MA, USA, 1999.
14. Puffet, N.K.; Gavin, C. *Predictors of Program Outcome & Recidivism at the Bronx Misdemeanor Domestic Violence Court*; Center for Court Innovation: New York, NY, USA, 2004.
15. Hilton, N.Z.; Harris, G.T.; Popham, S.; Lang, C. Risk Assessment among Incarcerated Male Domestic Violence Offenders. *Crim. Justice Behav.* **2010**, *37*, 815–832. [CrossRef]
16. Loinaz, I. Typologies, risk and recidivism in partner-violent men with the B-SAFER: A pilot study. *Psychol. Crime Law* **2014**, *20*, 183–198. [CrossRef]
17. Steinman, M. Lowering Recidivism Among Men Who Batter Women. *J. Police Sci. Adm.* **1990**, *17*, 124–132.
18. Kropp, P.R.; Hart, S.D. The Spousal Assault Risk Assessment (SARA) Guide: Reliability and Validity in Adult Male Offenders. *Law Hum. Behav.* **2000**, *24*, 101–118. [CrossRef]
19. Williams, K.; Houghton, A. Assessing the risk of domestic violence re-offending: A validation study. *Law Hum. Behav.* **2004**, *28*, 437–455. [CrossRef] [PubMed]
20. Hilton, N.Z.; Harris, G.T.; Rice, M.E.; Lang, C.; Cormier, C.A.; Lines, K.J. A Brief Actuarial Assessment for the Prediction of Wife Assault Recidivism: The Ontario Domestic Assault Risk Assessment. *Psychol. Assess.* **2004**, *16*, 267–275. [CrossRef] [PubMed]
21. Hilton, N.Z.; Harris, G.T.; Rice, M.E.; Houghton, R.E.; Eke, A.W. An in-depth actuarial assessment for wife assault recidivism: The domestic violence risk appraisal guide. *Law Hum. Behav.* **2008**, *32*, 150–163. [CrossRef] [PubMed]
22. Straus, M.A.; Hamby, S.L.; Boney-McCoy, S.; Sugarman, D. *The Personal and Relationship Profile (PRP Form P2)*; University of New Hampshire: Durham, NH, USA, 1999.
23. Campbell, J.C. Nursing Assessment of Risk of Homicide for Battered Women. *Adv. Nurs. Sci.* **1986**, *8*, 36–51. [CrossRef]
24. Fahlman, S. Faster-learning variation on backpropagation: An empirical study. In *Proceedings of the 1998 Connectionist Models Summer School*; Morgan Kaufmann Publishers: Los Altos, CA, USA, 1998.
25. Rumelhart, D.E.; McClelland, J. *Explorations in the Micro-Structure of Cognition, Vol. I and II*; The PDP Research Group, Ed.; The MIT Press: Cambridge, MA, USA, 1986.
26. Sprecher, A.G.; Muelleman, R.L.; Wadman, M.C. A Neural Network Model Analysis to Identify Victims of Intimate Partner Violence. *Am. J. Emerg. Med.* **2004**, *22*, 87–89. [CrossRef] [PubMed]
27. Pao, H. A Comparison of Neural Network and Multiple Regression Analysis in Modeling Campital Structure. *Expert Syst. Appl.* **2008**, *35*, 720–727. [CrossRef]

28. Barcelos-Tronto, I.; Da Silva, J.; Sant'Anna, N. Comparison of Artificial Neural Network and Regression Models in Software Effort Estimation. In Proceedings of the 2007 International Joint Conference on Neural Networks, Orlando, FL, USA, 12–17 August 2007; pp. 771–776.
29. Liew, P.L.; Lee, Y.C.; Lin, Y.C.; Lee, T.S.; Lee, W.J.; Wang, W.; Chien, C.W. Comparison of Artificial Neural Networks with Logistic Regression in Prediction of Gallbladder Disease among Obese Patients. *Dig. Liver Dis.* **2007**, *39*, 356–362. [CrossRef]
30. Ayer, T.; Chhatwal, J.; Alagoz, O.; Kahn, C.E.; Woods, R.; Burnside, E.S. Breast Cancer Risk Estimation with Artificial Neural Networks Revisited. *Cancer* **2010**, *116*, 3310–3321. [CrossRef]
31. Jaimes, F.; Farbiarz, D.A.; Martinez, C. Comparison between Logistic Regression and Neural Networks to Predict Death in Patients with Suspected Sepsis in the Emergency Room. *Crit. Care* **2005**, *9*, 150–156. [CrossRef]
32. Sargent, D.J. Comparison of Artificial Neural Networks with Other Statistical Approaches: Results from Medical Data Sets. *Cancer* **2001**, *15*, 91. [CrossRef]
33. Lawrence, J. *Introduction to Neural Networks, Design, Theory, and Applications*; California Scientific Software: Nevada City, CA, USA, 1994.
34. Wu, J.H.; Wang, G.L.; Li, X.M.; Yin, S.F. Comparison of BP Neural Network Model and and Logistic Regression in the Analysis of Influencing Factors of Violence in Hospitals. *Appl. Mech. Mater.* **2011**, *50*, 964–967. [CrossRef]
35. Grann, M.; Langstrom, N. Actuarial Assessment of Violence Risk: To Weigh or Not to Weigh. *Crim. Justice Behav.* **2007**, *34*, 22–36. [CrossRef]
36. Palocsay, S.; Wang, P.; Brookshire, W. Predicting Criminal Recidivism Using Neural Networks. *Socio-Econ. Plan. Sci.* **2000**, *34*, 271–284. [CrossRef]
37. Straus, M.A.; Hamby, S.L.; Boney-McCoy, S.; Sugarman, D.B. The Revised Conflict Tactics Scale (CTS2). *J. Fam. Issues* **1996**, *17*, 283–316. [CrossRef]
38. Spanier, G.B. Measuring Dyadic Adjustment: New Scales for Assessing the Quality of Marriage and Similar Dyads. *J. Marriage Fam.* **1976**, *38*, 15–28. [CrossRef]
39. Babcock, J.C.; Green, C.E.; Webb, S.A.; Yerington, T.P. Psychophysiological Profiles of Batterers: Autonomic Emotional Reactivity as It Predicts the Antisocial Spectrum of Behavior among Intimate Partner Abusers. *J. Abnorm. Psychol.* **2005**, *11*, 445–455. [CrossRef]
40. Babcock, J.C.; Green, C.E.; Webb, S.A.; Graham, K.H. A Second Failure to Replicate the Gottman et Al. *J. Fam. Psychol.* **2004**, *18*, 369–400.
41. Straus, M.A. Cross-Cultural Reliability and Validity of the Multidimensional Neglectful Behavior Scale Adult Recall Short Form. *Child Abuse Neglect* **2006**, *30*, 1257–1279. [CrossRef] [PubMed]
42. Straus, M.A. Dominance and symmetry in partner violence by male and female university students in 32 nations. *Child. Youth Serv. Rev.* **2008**, *30*, 252–275. [CrossRef]
43. Straus, M.A. The National Context Effect: An Empirical Test of the Validity of Cross-National Research Using Unrepresentative Samples. *Cross-Cult. Res.* **2009**, *43*, 183–205. [CrossRef]
44. Roehl, J.; O'Sullivan, C.; Webster, D.; Campbell, J. *Intimate Partner Violence Risk Assessment Validation Study: The RAVE Study Practitioner Summary and Recommendations: Validation of Tools for Assessing Risk from Violent Intimate Partners*; U.S. Department of Justice: Washington, DC, USA, 2005.
45. Cohen, J.; Zimmerman, S. Improved techniques for assessing the accuracy of recidivism prediction scales. In *H. John Heinz III School of Public Policy and Management*; Working Paper; Carnegie Mellon University: Pittsburgh, PA, USA, 1990.
46. Goring, H.; Baldwin, R.; Marriot, A.; Pratt, H.; Roberts, C. Validation of Short Screening Tests for Depression and Cognitive Impairment in Older Medically Ill Patients. *Int. J. Geriatr. Psychiatry* **2004**, *19*, 465–471. [CrossRef]
47. Cerulli, C.; Kothari, C.; Dichter, M.; Marcus, S.; Wiley, J.; Rhodes, K. Victim Participation in Intimate Partner Violence Prosecution. *Violence Against Women* **2014**, *20*, 539–560. [CrossRef]
48. Tu, J. Advantages and Disadvantages of Using Artificial Neural Networks versus Logistic Regression for Predicting Medical Outcomes. *J. Clin. Epidemiol.* **1996**, *49*, 1225–1231. [CrossRef]
49. Duh, M.; Walker, A.; Pagano, M.; Kronlund, K. Prediction and Cross-Validation of Neural Networks versus Logistic Regression: Using Hepatic Disorders as an Example. *Am. J. Epidemiol.* **1998**, *147*, 407–413. [CrossRef]

50. Hajmeer, M.N.; Basheer, I.A. A Hybrid Bayesian–Neural Network Approach for Probabilistic Modeling of Bacterial Growth/No-Growth Interface. *Int. J. Food Microbiol.* **2003**, *82*, 233–243. [CrossRef]
51. Hagan, M.; King, S. Accuracy of Psychologists' short-term predictions of future criminal behavior among juveniles. *J. Offender Rehabil.* **1997**, *25*, 129–141. [CrossRef]
52. Clermont, G.; Angus, D.; DiRusso, S.; Griffin, M.; Linde-Zwirble, W. Predicting hospital mortality for patients in the intensive care unit: A comparison of artificial neural networks with logistic regression models. *Crit. Care Med.* **2001**, *29*, 291–296. [CrossRef]

© 2019 by the authors. Licensee MDPI, Basel, Switzerland. This article is an open access article distributed under the terms and conditions of the Creative Commons Attribution (CC BY) license (http://creativecommons.org/licenses/by/4.0/).

Article

The Challenges of Safety and Community Integration for Vulnerable Individuals

Melody M. Terras [1],*, Gillian Hendry [1] and Dominic Jarret [2]

1. Department Division of Psychology, University of the West of Scotland, Paisley PA1 2BE, UK; gillian.hendry@uws.ac.uk
2. North Ayrshire Health and Social Care Partnership, Irvine KA12 8EE, UK; dominic.jarrett@nhs.net
* Correspondence: melody.terras@uws.ac.uk

Received: 26 July 2019; Accepted: 22 November 2019; Published: 6 December 2019

Abstract: Although community inclusion brings a number of advantages for vulnerable individuals, it can also entail a range of challenges, and draws in issues of safety and security. This qualitative psychological study, therefore, aimed to explore the challenges being faced by two groups of vulnerable individuals: those with intellectual disabilities and dementia, and how these could be addressed in order to establish a community that is safe and welcoming for all. Interviews and focus groups were conducted with a range of community stakeholders—for instance, local businesses, residents, and individuals with intellectual disabilities, dementia and their carers—and data was thematically analysed to explore the issue of inclusion and participation particularly in relation to stigma and prejudice, self-worth, social isolation and feeling safe. As well as highlighting practical issues regarding inclusion and support, the work emphasised the psychological dimension, linking to a multi-faceted conception of community participation. While significant work is already addressing issues of risk and safety for vulnerable populations (such as "Keep Safe" schemes), the work described here leads to an alternative conceptualization, tied to notions of kindness in communities with a view to crafting communities capable of safely welcoming a wider variety of marginalized groups.

Keywords: community safety; intellectual disability; dementia; vulnerable adults; discrimination; inclusion; barriers to participation; psychological perceptions of safety; kindness; inclusive design

1. Introduction

Human beings have a basic need to belong, which causes them to affiliate, to join and be members of groups. Such affiliation results in successful connections to others, producing heightened self-esteem and self-worth [1]. Group affiliation not only brings benefits for individuals themselves, but can also afford opportunities to further shape the group and its surrounding community context. Almost 100 years ago, Dewey recognized that engaging citizens in meaningful participation in local practices and decisions that shaped their lives led to increased participation at a community level which protected and advanced citizens' interests within broader society [2]. Existing research also identifies a number of other advantages of community participation, such as health and social benefits [3], strengthening relationships between members [4], enhancing services and preventing crime [5].

Community participation has both a physical dimension, in terms of the engagement behaviour itself, and a psychological dimension which reflects motivational, emotional and attitudinal aspects. Sense of community i.e., feelings of membership or belongingness to a community group [4] is a fundamental psychological aspect of participation, and it is essential to the development and empowerment of local communities; especially those that are marginalized and disadvantaged [6]. Its absence presents a significant barrier to community participation, and brings to the fore concerns about safety and security, in both practical and socio-emotional terms, particularly in relation to marginalized groups; a significant issue which has been highlighted previously within the literature, e.g., [7–11]. The multi-faceted perspective on community participation, outlined above, provides a valuable lens through which to view the issues of safety and security for more vulnerable members of society. Previous research has focused on teaching road safety [12], first aid skills [13], and use of public transport [14,15]. However, such a multifarious perspective on community participation highlights the need to not only address these very real and practical issues, but also psychological ones, such as belongingness and sense of community. Existing research indicates that community perceptions of vulnerable populations can play a role in marginalization [16], and vulnerable groups can be more susceptible to harm due to their minority status [17] and becoming "lost" in the community [8]. Encouragingly, the importance of social connectedness is reflected in a variety of government policies within the UK. For example, the Scottish Government's first strategy in 2018 aimed at tackling social isolation and building stronger communities makes specific recommendations to address stigma and discrimination, improve opportunities for people to connect and further empower communities themselves [18].

Everyone has the right to access their local community, though for some people this can be more challenging than others: individuals with an intellectual disability are at greater risk of isolation within their communities [19]. Individuals with an intellectual disability are "one of the most marginalized groups in Western society, experiencing severe personal, social and institutional abjection and discrimination" [20] (p. 107). Heiman and Shemesh [11] report that, compared to students without intellectual disabilities, students with intellectual disabilities report more cyber victimization, and a plethora of research has identified that people with intellectual disabilities are at an increased risk of abuse in differing forms [10,21,22]. Available evidence indicates that rates of social and community inclusion for people with an intellectual disability generally are low [23]. Individuals, especially those with mild disabilities, have more negative perceptions of key aspects of the environment such as whether they like the neighbourhood and perceived community spirit; access to shops, education and health care, and feelings of safety and fear of crime [9].

Insight into how inclusion may be promoted comes from the observational work of Craig and Bigby (2015) who examined how community groups respond to and support the participation of people with a moderate level of intellectual impairment. Findings indicate that successful community participation is characterised by equality i.e., the individual with a learning disability feels and is perceived as an equal and full member of the group, is engaged in a high degree of co-operative working within the group and that membership is rewarding for all members [24].

Inclusion brings challenges for all concerned: the person with an intellectual disability may be concerned about participating; support staff and family carers may want to protect them from discrimination and therefore restrict opportunities; and there may be practical challenges in terms of time and resources to support the activity. Community groups too face challenges both practically in terms of risk management and socially in terms of attitudes and beliefs as the inclusion of an individual with an intellectual disability may change the dynamic and initial shared vision of the group [23]. Therefore, further research is required to examine community views and community responses to the inclusion of people with an intellectual disability generally, and to explore the views, experiences and challenges that community participation brings for people with an intellectual disability and their carers.

People with dementia represent another vulnerable population for whom the advantages of community participation are increasingly being recognised. Loneliness is a significant issue for people with dementia, as noted by Moyle and colleagues [25]. In their exploration of the experiences of people with dementia and those caring for them, they found that carers attributed the socially isolating behaviour of peers to a lack of understanding of dementia, and a fear regarding how to communicate or interact. Bowes et al. [26] identify that participating in community leisure activities has benefits beyond those associated with remaining physically active when an individual develops dementia, as they can promote both social and mental well-being. International work has further underlined the impact of stigma and lack of understanding [27]. These issues are also familiar to people with intellectual disabilities, and the ways in which society can at times fail to recognise their rights is mirrored in the experiences of people with dementia. The Dementia Engagement and Empowerment Project, for example, highlights the rights of people with dementia to have access to information they can understand, and makes recommendations in this regard [28] which share much with guidance around accessible materials for people with intellectual disabilities. Data also indicates the relatively low rates of inclusion for people with dementia. For instance, Morgan et al. [29] identified eight barriers that individuals with dementia face when accessing community-based services, such as lack of awareness, challenges in service delivery, and beliefs and attitudes: the same factors have been identified in relation to people with intellectual disabilities [7]. Snyder and colleagues [30] termed people's feelings of decreased self-worth in being part of the community as "devaluation", and in their review of literature on the needs of people with dementia, van der Roest et al. [31] identified that the most frequently reported needs of people with dementia are to be accepted and respected as they are, which is not necessarily realistic in terms of being safe and secure in the community. Indeed, there is a plethora of literature focusing on the stigmatic and prejudiced attitudes towards people with an intellectual disability or dementia (e.g., [32–35]) which undoubtedly contributes to diminished feelings of safety and inclusion in the community.

Existing research illustrates the extent to which both dementia and intellectual disability populations experience similar physical and psychological barriers in terms of safe community participation. Although the available literature indicates that increased community participation raises a number of challenges for adults with an intellectual disability or dementia as distinct populations, a detailed understanding of community participation and safety issues and how they overlap for these populations remains underexplored and unspecified. The project reported below aims to address this issue by considering the rich contextualized insights from a community-based qualitative study. The opportunity arose to work with a community who were motivated to make their community more inclusive for all and who were keen to understand the barriers to participation and the challenges to safety and security it entails. Similar to work in Ireland which sought to use a Universal Design Approach to produce guidance around dementia friendly hospitals [36], the work described here sought to use the experiences of people with intellectual disabilities and/or dementia and those who care for them to generate insights that would help craft a community that was safer and more welcoming for all. The specific aims for the study were to identify the following:

- What are the key issues that people with an intellectual disability and/or dementia, and their carers, face in community settings?
- How do community members perceive the needs of people with an intellectual disability and/or dementia?
- What support is required to accommodate the needs of individuals with an intellectual disability and dementia within the safer and friendlier community initiative?

2. Materials and Methods

In this section we report the finding of a community-based qualitative study, based in a small town in the West of Scotland that was interested in making their community more inclusive and safe for all community members, especially vulnerable individuals such as those with dementia and/or an intellectual disability.

2.1. Participants and Recruitment

Before recruitment commenced university ethical approval was sought and received. Participants were self-identifying and recruited via convenience and snowball sampling: existing community groups (e.g., carers/support groups), and individual carers of vulnerable individuals known to the members of the community group leading the initiative were contacted and asked if they had members or friends who might also be interested in participating. Participants were also recruited more generally within the community in response to the opportunity to participate in a community engagement exercise advertised via local community links. Recruitment snowballed as other community stakeholders heard about the project and were keen to be included, resulting in interviews and focus groups being conducted with community members with and without any form of disability, local businesses, carers, volunteers, local councillors, church groups, community group leaders and charitable organisations. Definitions of intellectual disability have habitually made reference to IQ criteria along with other defining features. However, a more pragmatic concept of learning disability, less bound by IQ criteria, is beginning to emerge. Within the recent Learning Disability (the preferred term for intellectual disability in Scotland) Strategy published by the Scottish Government, the definition used (and one developed with the involvement of people with intellectual disability themselves) was: "A learning disability is significant and lifelong. It starts before adulthood and affects the person's development. This means that a person with a learning disability will be likely to need help to understand information, learn skills and live a fulfilling life. Some people with learning disabilities will also have healthcare needs and require support to communicate." ([37], p. 9).

With regard to dementia, within the World Health Organisation global action plan on dementia, it is described as: "an umbrella term for several diseases that are mostly progressive, affecting memory, other cognitive abilities and behaviour, and that interfere significantly with a person's ability to maintain the activities of daily living". ([38], p. 2).

For the purposes of this work, participants were recruited as outlined above from a range of community services or local support groups for people with intellectual disability, or people with dementia. No formal assessment of intellectual disability or dementia was undertaken by the project team, or required to be evidenced and so, in effect, we accepted people as self-identifying as having an intellectual disability and/or dementia.

Thirty-five participants were recruited including older adults with dementia and/or an intellectual disability (N = 5), carers/support workers for people with dementia and/or an intellectual disability (N = 9), community and charity group leaders and volunteers, representatives from local businesses and church groups, and other interested community members (N = 21). Thirteen one to one interviews (with eight carers/support workers for adults with an intellectual disability and three individuals with dementia) and two focus groups (one focus group with 21 community stakeholders, and one focus group with one support worker from a local charity and two individuals with an intellectual disability who attended that group on a regular basis) were conducted.

2.2. Data Collection and Analysis

Discussions with vulnerable adults and carers/support workers were focused by using a semi-structured interview schedule that probed issues such as the extent and experience of community participation, preferences for community participation, barriers to community participation, and the support required to enable increased participation in community events. Discussions with community stakeholders were also focused using a semi-structured interview schedule that contained trigger questions to probe issues such as their perceptions of the needs and abilities of vulnerable individuals, barriers to community participation and what support (in terms of education, training and adaptation) is required to increase the safe participation of vulnerable individuals within the community.

All discussions were audio-recorded, transcribed verbatim and thematically analysed [39]; a method which is in keeping with existing research with similar populations [40,41].

Data collection totalled 472 min. Individual interviews ranged from 10–53 (average: 29) minutes and focus groups ranged from 46–53 (average: 49) minutes in length. In accordance with ethical clearance all participants were fully informed of the aims of the study and their right to withdraw (both verbally and via an information sheet) and gave signed consent to participate and were debriefed after the study (both verbally and via a debrief sheet). Participants' identities were protected by using pseudonyms, and only the named authors had access to the recordings and transcripts, which were stored securely.

3. Results

The following section outlines the key themes concerning the integration of vulnerable individuals in the community illustrated with quotes from various community members. These themes focus on (1) stigma and prejudice, (2) self-worth, (3) social isolation, and (4) feeling safe. In general, these themes illustrate barriers to community inclusion. However, participants also reflected on how some of these difficulties may be overcome and identified a range of potential enablers consisting of the provision of practical and emotional support captured by the theme of (5) supporting community participation.

3.1. Stigma and Prejudice

Erving Goffman [42] (p. 3) is credited for his seminal work regarding stigma, defining it as, "[an] attribute that is deeply discrediting and that reduces the bearer from a whole and usual person to a tainted and discounted one". The term was used frequently by participants as a barrier to the development of an inclusive community, and there was reference to the fact that other people's attitudes have an impact on the lives of people with an intellectual disability and dementia, highlighting the need for understanding and learning on the part of the community:

> "I don't know if there's just not the understanding there, the stigma, I don't know, but I've had a few people say certain places they go they feel a bit even more isolated because they've made an effort to go along to an activity and then they're not really included in it". (Support worker for an individual with an intellectual disability).

It is clear from the above quote that there is a direct link between stigma and inclusion, or lack thereof. The participant identifies that although there are community opportunities for the more vulnerable members of the community, they still may not be included: that in theory there are opportunities, but in practice there is still exclusion. However, participants, too, realised that this may not be a barrier that is specific to the current community, but representative of a wider problem: a finding consistent with existing research [43]. For example,

> "You're always going to get people in communities that are out unfortunately to target vulnerable people but that's everywhere". (Support worker for an individual with an intellectual disability).
> "I think you never get away from the fact that some people are biased ... there's always people who are gonna treat them differently, but as long as they're being treated well by the most people, I think that's the important part". (Community Group Leader).

The above quotes demonstrate that the targeting of vulnerable individuals appears to be universally accepted: it is found "everywhere". This normalisation is concerning as it suggests a pervasive problem in society, and even though it is mentioned that "most people" treat such groups well, it suggests that more community education is required to ensure that people with intellectual disabilities and dementia are not denied opportunities to engage in the community, and are supported to do so. One study, for instance, demonstrated that disabled youths described feeling safe in their community only half as often as nondisabled peers [44]. This highlights the importance of making spaces safe for individuals with vulnerabilities, which is the whole premise of dementia friendly communities: a place or culture in which people with dementia can be empowered, supported and included in society [45–48]. Alzheimer Scotland determines that a dementia friendly community is made up of the whole community; people who are committed to working together and helping people with dementia to remain a part of their community and not become apart from it [49]. This is particularly important in the current study, as exclusion was identified as an issue for the more vulnerable members of the community. However, that is not to say that only individuals with dementia benefit from such cultures: they can be beneficial for all [50].

3.2. Self-Worth

Issues of prejudice and stigma can be an even greater barrier to safety and community participation if they are manifested as hate crime. Traditionally focused on religion, race and sexuality, disability hate crime is a relatively more recent topic [51]. Participants identified that for the more vulnerable members of the community, there was evidence of "mate crime"; a play on the term "hate crime", it refers to a specific form of hate crime against disabled people, predominantly those with intellectual disabilities [52].

> "It's not just disability hate crime, there's mate crime as well and it's where friendships are struck up because there are a lot of people with an intellectual disability in the area that are vulnerable that don't have support". (Support worker for an individual with an intellectual disability).
>
> "There's people that can take advantage of people with an intellectual disability as in, 'oh they don't get support in their support hours' and maybe target them for like mate crime, you know, 'oh, I've not got any money today'". (Support worker for an individual with an intellectual disability).

In the above quotes, there is acknowledgement of mate crime happening to some of the individuals in the community under consideration. It is identified that friendships are established with vulnerable people who do not have support, on the proviso that they give them money, with such exploitation being identified as a common feature of the "crime" [53]. Individuals with intellectual disabilities may not realise that they may be taken advantage of in such a way, and even if they do, research has shown that disabled people generally face barriers to reporting abuse (e.g., [10,54–56]). Grundy [57] details an initiative focused on mate crime: "Safety Net" was established in 2009, aiming to prevent the exploitation of people with intellectual disabilities by those claiming to be their friends. The project reported the main finding to be that people with an intellectual disability can struggle to recognize when they are being exploited [58]; a finding replicated in further research [52].

This has clear links to the safety of the more vulnerable community members, however, feeling unsafe in the community is not only linked to social factors within the community and the incidence of crime, it can also be attributed to psychological resources such as fear of crime, motivation and low self-worth, which may also function as barriers to community participation. O'Rourke and colleagues [59] discussed how people with an intellectual disability have a desire to engage more in community activities, and indeed, respondents in this study spoke about the benefits that are obtained for individuals by being included in the community, as detailed below:

> "Feeling wanted and needed and for themselves, just to get out". (Carer of someone with Dementia).

Participants regarded inclusion as important as it was related to self-worth, which was also identified as a barrier to inclusion, in that if individuals had feelings of low self-worth, they are less likely to want to be actively part of the community. This presents somewhat of a dilemma: individuals do not have the self-worth to feel a valued part of the community, but not being part of the community may enhance the feelings of low self-worth. Furthermore, lack of participation reduces the opportunity to become aware of the actual nature of the community and this lack of understanding and experience may help reinforce negative perceptions of the risks and increase concerns over safety that further restrict motivation to engage with the community. This then puts vulnerable community members at risk of social isolation, as detailed in the next section.

3.3. Social Isolation

Although increased community involvement is assumed to entail a degree of risk as detailed by aforementioned research (e.g., [31–34]), a number of community stakeholders identified social isolation as a major risk due to a lack of community participation. Although some of this risk may be attributed to geographical location, much is due to social factors. Research suggests that rates of social and community inclusion for people with an intellectual disability generally are low [23,60] and that the barriers faced by people with intellectual disabilities in their everyday lives indicate the importance of social knowledge and skills to help facilitate social integration, the role of support, and the impact of community factors such as lack of amenities and attitudes [7]. Consider the following:

> "Isolation must be hell, and to feel needed and, you know, it must be awful being lonely and seeing nobody from day to a day, and there must be quite a few like that". (Carer of an individual with Dementia).

It was worrisome that isolation was being identified in the current project as a major risk factor: there are people within the community that do not see other people on a day to day basis or are not able to pursue friendships. Despite isolation being a huge concern amongst all participants—and being identified as a problem for the community—participants identified that support is needed to tackle the issue:

> "You see so many of these people that are in isolation and you think, 'I wish there was a way just to get them altogether', but again it would be about they'd need lots of support". (Support worker for an individual with an intellectual disability).

Often, community participation is linked to leisure, and a number of barriers to participation in leisure activities for such vulnerable groups were identified. Such barriers may be intrinsic in nature; attributable to characteristics of the individual such as communication and social skills and degree of dependency on caregivers, or more environmental factors such as perceived attitudes of others and more practical issues such as access [61]. Here, too, constraints often interact and even when practical issues are addressed such as the availability of transport, social barriers such as the attitudes of carers remain [62]. Research has also examined how dementia can restrict participation in leisure activities which also highlights the importance of environmental factors concerning accessibility in relation to transport, toilets, venues and carer influences concerning fear of the person with dementia getting lost and the restriction choice of activities [43], as detailed by the following:

> "If they didn't have the support to go to them, you know, they probably wouldn't be able to access them. Sometimes as well if there's things on they might want to go to, but if it's out-with their support hours, that might be a barrier". (Support worker for an individual with an intellectual disability).

Despite such barriers, community members do recognise opportunities to take part in community initiatives:

> (MyBus: door to door transport) "so you could be picked up from your house, taken to the shop and then picked up again as a group which I think it sometimes—people feel safer that way". (Support worker for an individual with an intellectual disability).
> (The local group for people with intellectual disabilities) "are gonny start working on a wee drama now … about keeping safe in the local community, so any new community initiatives, if I can support it with our guys (I will)". (Support worker for an individual with an intellectual disability).
> "it's about having safer communities, so having an approach that as communities we're aware. There's these initiatives going on but it's all under the same umbrella; it's to make everybody feel safe in their local communities". (Support worker for an individual with an intellectual disability).

As noted by Hall [63], community involvement is one aspect of social inclusion that enhances the quality of life of people with intellectual disabilities. However, research indicates that integration requires a collaborative effort: the individual with the additional needs must adapt to the community, but the community also needs to be responsive to their needs [19]. The Scottish Commission for Learning Disability [64] highlights a similar point, in that individuals supporting people with intellectual disabilities into mainstream community groups will help them to adapt to the group, and vice versa. Exiting research also indicates that successful participation is characterised by equality in that the individual with an intellectual disability feels and is perceived as an equal and full member of the group—as discussed in the previous them—and is engaged in a high degree of co-operative working within the group [24]. Research has also demonstrated that disabled people do not always wish to be associated with other disabled people [65], however, contrasting work has shown that disabled individuals can feel a greater sense of belonging when around others also like them, and that spending time in places that feel safe is a key element for the maintenance of friendships between disabled people [66], as detailed below in the next theme.

3.4. Feeling Safe

One striking finding that was clear from the people we spoke to was that feeling safe is often dependent on other people. Indeed, Gerber [67] reviewed the different factors that can contribute positively to quality of life for people with intellectual disabilities and for successful adjustment in the community and identified the important role that peers and family play in offering social support. Consider the following:

> (when asked if she thinks her mother feels safe) "I think so because there's neighbours that look out for her curtains aren't open, you know, so, knocking the door". (Carer of an individual with Dementia).

> "We are lucky, when we're out and about, people help". (Support worker for an individual with an intellectual disability).

> (Talking about her sheltered accommodation) "you've got people looking after you ... a perfect place". (Person with Dementia).

Above, we see the participant discuss how her assurances of her mother's safety comes from her mother's neighbours who will check in with her mother if anything seems out of the ordinary (i.e., her curtains not being open). Similarly, another participant talks about feeling "lucky" due to other people helping when they are out in the community, whilst a person with dementia talks about the security she feels from the people looking after her. Research has similarly identified the importance of strong commitment by community members to support more vulnerable individuals in rural places [68]; indeed, this focus on support is mentioned as one of the defining features of a dementia-friendly community by Alzheimer's Society [69], but returning to the focus on isolation, consider the individuals who are not able to contribute to the community, as detailed in the following quote:

> "I also think as well that those that are socially isolated: do we know we are connecting with them? I'm very conscious in terms of community engagement that I see a lot of people—a lot of people—and there's a real will to join in things, but I see a lot of the same people and they're doing shed loads of work but I worry that the people I don't see—who am I not seeing?". (Community Stakeholder).

A key finding from existing research is the importance of support staff/carers for individuals with an intellectual disability and those with dementia (e.g., [19,70]): this is absolutely crucial, as without support and care, some individuals with an intellectual disability and/or dementia would face considerable difficulties with many routine daily activities, as well as participating in the community [71].

Shalock et al. [72] identified the twenty-five most commonly reported indicators of quality of life which include community integration and participation, community roles and social supports: it is evident from the data set that without support from others, individuals with dementia and intellectual disabilities would be even more isolated than they currently are. In this, they are no different from any other member of society, for all that the nature of that support may differ in terms of scale and intensity. Indeed, the increasing profile attached to isolation issues within Government policy [18,73] further highlights the basic need for connection that all community members share.

3.5. Supporting Community Participation

Community members also identified a range of enablers that may facilitate increased community participation. The enablers identified mostly related to support, either physical in the form of improved transport, more accessible information and having someone available to assist and provide both practical and emotional support. For example, the issue of accessing transport to enable individuals to participate in a wider range of community events was discussed at length, particularly as access to transport was currently perceived as a constraint. For example:

> "She stays in a little village eight miles out of town, there's a lot less opportunities there, and because transport becomes a logistics thing". (Carer of an individual with Dementia).

> "I think it's transport we need—better transport". (Carer of an individual with Dementia).

The above quotes are just a sample of the responses concerning how the lack of transport can act as barrier, but improved transport can function as an enabler. This is in keeping with existing research which highlights the significance of transport as an enabler to community participation [74]. Although there may be opportunities for vulnerable individuals to contribute to community activities, if they cannot physically get there, then the opportunity cannot be maximised. It is important to remember that the simple practical availability of transport may not be sufficient, and individuals may require support to use transport due to cognitive difficulties, money troubles, or low confidence [75].

Another facet of "support" is the enabling aspect of being able to access information. Participants in this study clearly reflected on existing practice and highlighted the need for information about community happenings to be delivered in a way that is accessible to all. The fact that there is variability in how people share and receive information was also noted and the importance of recognising these individual differences to minimise the risk of marginalisation for all vulnerable groups [20]. For instance,

> "I don't know that we always present information in the best way for people". (Support worker for an individual with an intellectual disability).

> "The communication needs to be put out in different ways so that everybody knows ... Facebook will get one generation, newspapers will get another generation but you're not going to get your person with dementia who's stuck in the house on a Facebook page or reading the local paper, so you're not—to me it's just simple: you're not going to get them". (Support worker for an individual with an intellectual disability).

When discussing the issue of community inclusion consideration was given to the importance of raising awareness within the wider population of the needs of individuals with dementia and a learning disability in order to foster increased inclusion within the community, as evidenced by the following:

> "I think as an area we need to maybe raise a bit more awareness among young people". (Community Stakeholder).
> The community needs) "to be more caring, considerate, and I think people've got to learn what it's all about, and understand it a bit more". (Carer of an individual with Dementia).

The importance of awareness is recognized as being crucial for the community inclusion of individuals with dementia [31]. However, awareness although it may be necessary may not be sufficient. For example, in relation to people with an intellectual disability as research indicates that integration for people with a learning disability requires a collaborative effort: the individual with a learning disability needs to adapt to the community, but the community also need to be responsive to their needs [19]. Interestingly this was recognised by respondents who also identified that not only was community effort and awareness required, but also that people with dementia and a learning disability need to be aware of the community happenings:

"Is there a better way of advertising what there is for people? I don't know how you target the folk individually, but how do we make sure people are getting the information about what we're saying?". (Support worker for an individual with an intellectual disability).

"Even letting people know that's on and things: it doesn't matter how many posters you put up, it's sometimes difficult to make contact with everybody". (Community Group Leader).

Participants also recognized the need to provide more opportunities for participation with the very practical suggestions of facilitating more scope for involvement not just for vulnerable individuals but for the whole community, whether that be through work placements, buddies to go shopping with, or community events, offer interesting ways to break down these barriers. For example:

"I think more opportunities for them to be involved in their communities, whether it's volunteering, whether it's wee work placements. Just being able to be involved in initiatives if there's clubs, if there's activities going on". (Support worker for an individual with an intellectual disability).

"I was suggesting like a buddy system in supermarkets/a befriender, a buddy, and transport to get to places". (Support worker for an individual with an intellectual disability).
"For our group of people, anything arts and crafts and anything music ... even if they could do something like all year round, like even set up a tea dance almost, so it was open to everybody, not just our focus". (Support worker for an individual with an intellectual disability).

"I'm sure there was a lot of more things that they could add to the town that's already here to help other people and I just feel there's a definite lack of further thinking". (Carer of an individual with Dementia).

Participants recognized that there is a clear gap between the kinds of opportunities that are sought, and the ability to put them in place. It is essential that this area is addressed as research demonstrates that participating in leisure activities has benefits beyond those associated with remaining physically active but also promotes social and mental well-being [70].

Existing research illustrates the important role of support staff and carers in enabling the community participation for individuals with a learning disability and those with dementia [19] and their importance was also recognised and valued by participants in this study:

"You can't just put ten people with a learning disability in a room and expect them all to learn the same way as you or I; they need support". (Support worker for an individual with an intellectual disability).

4. Discussion

The project findings highlight a range of psychological factors and practical influences on the safety and community participation of people with intellectual disabilities and/or dementia. Stigma and lack of awareness within the community presented significant barriers, which are by no means unique to the populations considered here, but which carry further significance as a result of their particular vulnerability and potentially considerable support needs. As an enabler and consequence of community participation, self-worth has a significant contribution to make to the overall wellbeing of individuals. Yet as highlighted here, its absence can present a significant barrier to that participation, and increase the risk of social isolation within the community. This was a very real issue for participants within the project, which further highlights the importance of the crucial role played by support from others in generating feelings of safety and enabling participation.

Responses to this complex interplay of issues are varied, but a particular approach highlighted by participants within this study was the promotion of "Keep Safe" schemes. These community initiatives work with a network of businesses such as shops, libraries and cafes who have agreed to make their premises a Keep Safe place for people to go if they feel frightened, distressed or are the victim of crime when out in the community. Keep Safe places are identified by displaying a sticker in the premises' window and are listed online [76]. Research has demonstrated that people with an intellectual disability often report observing the community instead of being part of it [77], and so such initiatives allow individuals to engage with the community, and also have the safety net of certain places they can go if they feel vulnerable. Similarly, research has identified that at some point in their disease process, people with dementia will have a "missing" incident and be unable to safely return to their care setting [78], at which point having established and identifiable places of safety to go to will be of the utmost importance. Participants in the current study identified the potential value of Keep Safe locations within their community. A recent report reviewing the Keep Safe initiative identified that, of 660 responses from a wider community survey, 94% thought that the Keep Safe initiative was worthwhile; 84% highlighted that it had made them more aware of disability hate crime and harassment; and 82% were more likely to report incidents of suspected hate crime [79]. Recent research has also explored the concept of "self-building safe havens", demonstrating that individuals with intellectual disabilities are themselves finding and negotiating welcome spaces in their neighbourhoods, and reclaiming the welcoming communities' agenda [80].

While "Keep Safe" schemes definitely have much to offer as regards further enabling community participation, the multi-faceted perspective highlighted previously encourages the exploration of other routes. The promotion of "Keep Safe" schemes are welcome steps towards addressing some of the barriers discussed here, yet they remain partial solutions delivered in ways which acknowledge and are limited by the status quo, for example, in being inherently risk oriented approaches.

The findings from this study offer a more positive means of conceptualizing and promoting inclusion, with a number of participants discussing how sensitivity and awareness of needs of vulnerable individuals contributes to feelings of actual and perceived safety. For example. one participant spoke about people being helpful when they were "out and about"; another participant discussed the benefits of a vulnerable relative having neighbours who would look out for them, and another participant spoke about the need for the community to be "more caring, considerate". The recognition of helping and caring as factors in facilitating safety and inclusion opens up the opportunity to consider the role of kindness, at the individual and community level. The multi-faceted perspective on inclusion introduced previously can apply here as: Knafo-Noam et al. (2015) describe how the complex array of positive behaviours displayed by humans, which they refer to as "prosociality", encompasses behavioural, attitudinal and emotional elements [81]. As well as reflecting this conceptual link, a focus on kindness also provides a practical link into current activity regarding community and service development.

Kindness as a concept invites a variety of definitions and approaches to describing and measuring it are still evolving [82]. There is, however, a growing body of evidence outlining the positive impact of acts of kindness at an individual level, to the extent of describing the neurological changes associated with their commitment [83]. While there has been recognition of a need for kindness to figure more explicitly in public policy [84], the related concept of compassion has an established place both as a potential mechanism for improving professional practice [85,86], and as a tool for change promoted in policy (for example, within the Compassion in Practice vision and strategy document produced by the English Department of Health (2012) [87], and the Compassionate Connections learning resources produced by NHS Education Scotland [88]). The notion of kindness as a relevant focus of explicit consideration is also increasingly emergent, linked not only to research based enquiry such as that outlined previously, but also high profile, practical examples of community change, such as the various strands of activity taking place as part of the Compassionate Inverclyde programme [89] which focuses on what the authors describe as "enabling ordinary people to do ordinary things for ordinary people" [89]. This includes the provision of conversation cafes, the provision of boxes of food stuffs and other resources for people coming home from hospital and the delivery of a programme of support to school pupils and others exploring the benefits of being kind to yourself and others.

Recent work by the Carnegie Foundation [90] further highlights the potential of kindness as an alternative perspective on risk and inclusion; one which is broader in its vision and has clear links to the psychological dimensions of community safety and participation—stigma, self-worth, and isolation—highlighted by this study. The Carnegie Foundation examined the place of kindness within communities, how it is realized, and how it can be promoted, and highlighted a range of barriers to kindness, including concerns about personal risk (what will happen when we open up and interact with others); regulation (the focus of organizations of managing risk through policy and regulation); professionalism (the perceived dominance of the "dispassionate professional" ideal); and performance management (measuring what we can, as opposed to what matters). The response of the Carnegie Foundation to these barriers [90] included leaders and government empowering people to act in kindness, and making it easier to do. Crucially, they also speak about the need to think and talk about kindness, with the consequence that this in itself will encourage kinder action.

The work of the Carnegie Foundation and others, combined with the existing evidence base around kindness and prosocial behaviour more generally, provides a significant conceptual and practical resource for further exploring the role of kindness with regard to inclusion. As suggested by the responses of participants within the project described here, there is a clear link between concerns about kindness within communities, and issues of safety and inclusion with regard to marginalized populations. This is particularly true when viewed in light of the psychological aspects of safety and community participation highlighted within the current work, and the role of issues such as confidence and self-worth as enablers for inclusion.

A potential obstacle to the adoption of kindness as a focus for community development may be that how this can be achieved is perhaps less readily tangible than actions linked to notions of risk (such as the promotion of "Keep Safe" schemes). Yet, as a long-term destination, guiding development of inclusively designed services and communities, greater kindness seems to be an aspiration worth investing in. While the promotion of kindness in a community and service context is inherently positive, the responses of participants within the work described here highlights the need to retain sight of marginalized groups such as those with intellectual disabilities and dementia while doing so. Indeed, the current authors would argue that basing any such activity around a consideration of those groups in the first place, should be a priority.

A kindness-oriented approach to the development of inclusive communities has a further advantage in providing a unifying framework for considering all members of the community. As noted earlier, vulnerable individuals (regardless of source e.g., dementia or an intellectual disability) seem to encounter similar challenges to safety when engaging in the community, and it may be beneficial to adopt a more global approach that seeks to accommodate the needs of all, as opposed to developing specific responses to the needs of specific groups of individuals. Communities should be more inclusive in general and thereby be able to meet the needs of all members. The dementia-friendly communities movement has a profile and momentum which has the potential to benefit many, if it is developed with deliberate attention being paid to its potential for cross-cutting benefits. The same holds true in relation to work focused on people with intellectual disabilities. As noted in the previously cited work from the Scottish Commission for Learning Disability [64] (p. 6) "if the learning disability movement joined with other movements to advocate for a place-based approach across Scotland, the impact would be transformational". Arguably, it is in the promotion of this synergy that the greatest potential lies for addressing community safety issues in a way which will benefit a range of marginalized groups.

A further mechanism for facilitating that synergy, which draws in both physical and psychological aspects of community participation, is the Inclusive Design paradigm. Inclusive Design (or the similar label, Design for all) provides an existing option which encourages the exploration of design issues with a view to accommodating a broad range of needs and abilities. The British Design Council describes Inclusive Design as aiming to remove of barriers that create undue effort and separation, thereby enabling everyone to participate equally, confidently and independently in everyday activities [91]. As such, it has much to offer in terms of enabling individuals, thereby building self-worth, which, as highlighted by the present study, is a critical resource in respect to safety concerns and community participation. While the project around which the present article is built identified a significant crossover with regard to the concerns of and barriers experienced by people with intellectual disabilities, and those with dementia (e.g., transport access; the experience of stigma; lack of accessible information on community opportunities; lack of awareness within the community), as the above quote suggests, it is in a broader vision that the most potential for progress may lie. Inclusive Design has the potential to accommodate that breadth of vision.

Inclusive Design is a clear priority within the private sector, but the extent to which it is consistently and meaningfully realized within the broader community and public sector is debatable. Collaboration with the community as part of the work described here highlighted the potential in creating new opportunities for engagement and exposure, to overcome prevalent preconceptions, and build greater confidence in marginalized groups. It may be that a critical part of this exposure/engagement relates to those specialist services supporting groups such as people with intellectual disabilities, or dementia. Professional identity is a powerful motivator for all, and for those working within specialist services, that professional identity is frequently closely tied to the identity of the individuals they work with, as perceived by the service. Inclusive, safe communities demand a lowering of barriers and divisions, yet all too often, services seem to be built around the preservation of some of those divisions.

Although it is anticipated that the conceptual frameworks for increasing community participation and the research findings discussed, with their emphasis on considering both the practical and psychological determinants of safe community participation, will promote debate, discussion, and help inform interventions; it is also essential to recognize the limitations of the current study. The small scale exploratory nature of this study entails some methodological implications that should be noted. The study was conducted in close collaboration with a community group who wished to make their community more inclusive and the study drew on these community links to facilitate recruitment. Doing do may have induced a degree of bias into the sample with participants potentially having favourable attitudes towards inclusion. However, this also brings the advantage of an informed perspective and the data itself shows how participants were able to critically reflect on existing initiatives and identify improvements for the future. The recruitment of vulnerable participants also presented a challenge to the research team and the final number of individuals interviewed was lower than anticipated. This may be attributable to a number of practical (not aware about the option to participate or lack of support to allow participation) and psychological factors (low self-esteem and/or not viewing themselves as a member of the community) many of which are a consequence of poor community integration in its own right. It is interesting to note that such factors were identified as barriers to inclusion by participants, with and without disabilities, within this study; and difficulties in engaging and recruiting individuals who are excluded or those of high risk of exclusion is a well-recognised challenge [92]. In order to maximise the voice of vulnerable individuals future research would benefit from supporting the interview process by the use of symbolic/photographic material and draw upon a "Talking Mats" approach where needed, to guide participants through the interview process at their pace and provide a supportive structure for their responding [93,94]. The provision of practical support, in terms of self-advocacy training, to help vulnerable participants articulate their views may also be beneficial [95]. Future research may also benefit from the use of a mixed methods approach that draws upon observational work of actual community activities to supplement interview and/or questionnaire data and build a more contextualized understanding of experiences of all community members [96].

5. Conclusions

Community participation has clear benefits at an individual and group level, yet these benefits are not equally available to all. Our findings indicate that similar barriers to safe community participation are experienced by individuals with an intellectual disability and dementia alike. Furthermore, the research findings indicate the importance of considering the role of psychological determinants such as prejudiced attitudes and stigma, self-worth and feelings of community belonging in relation to community safety and inclusion. As the current project outlined, people with intellectual disabilities and/or dementia are significantly disadvantaged in this respect, with concerns about safety (in various aspects) contributing largely to this. Individuals and communities can potentially benefit from targeted activity (e.g., Dementia Friendly Communities) or risk-oriented approaches (e.g., Keep Safe schemes). However, a perspective on participation and safety which draws in psychological as well as physical concerns creates an opportunity to address these issues from other, possibly more positive and inclusive perspectives. The role of kindness and inclusive design within communities are two such perspectives. Arguably, how they can be leveraged as mechanisms for promoting inclusion and participation for all, particularly for vulnerable groups such as those with intellectual disabilities and/or dementia, is an area that has been significantly under explored to date. Doing so has the potential to bridge the areas of community safety and asset-based community development, to the advantage of all community members.

Author Contributions: All three authors have contributed towards this paper: conceptualization; M.M.T., D.J., G.H.; methodology: M.M.T., D.J., G.H.; formal analysis: G.H., M.M.T., D.J.; investigation: G.H., M.M.T., D.J.; original draft preparation: G.H., M.M.T., D.J.; writing, review and editing: M.M.T., G.H., D.J.; project administration: M.M.T.

Funding: This research was funded by the RS MacDonald Charitable Trust (seedcorn grant) and distributed through host organization Alzheimer Scotland Centre for Policy and Practice, University of the West of Scotland.

Acknowledgments: We acknowledge and thank all the community members who engaged with the discussions and the community group leaders who are pioneering the development of safer and more inclusive practices within the community and who helped facilitate the recruitment of participants.

Conflicts of Interest: The authors declare no conflict of interest.

References

1. Baumeister, R.F.; Leary, M.R. The need to belong: Desire for interpersonal attachments as a fundamental human motivation. *Psychol. Bull.* **1995**, *117*, 497–529. [CrossRef] [PubMed]
2. Dewey, J. *The Public and Its Problems*; Holt: Oxford, UK, 1927.
3. Zakus, J.D.L.; Lysack, C.L. Revisiting community participation. *Health Policy Plan.* **1998**, *13*, 1–12. [CrossRef] [PubMed]
4. Manzo, L.C.; Perkins, D.D. Finding common ground: The importance of place attachment to community participation and planning. *J. Plan. Lit.* **2006**, *20*, 335–350. [CrossRef]
5. Chavis, D.M.; Wandersman, A. Sense of community in the urban environment: A catalyst for participation and community development. In *A Quarter Century of Community Psychology*; Revenson, T.A., Ed.; Springer: New York, NY, USA, 2002; pp. 265–292.
6. Florin, P.; Wandersman, A. An introduction to citizen participation, voluntary organizations, and community development: Insights for empowerment through research. *American J. Community psychol.* **1990**, *18*, 41–54. [CrossRef]
7. Abbott, S.; McConkey, R. The barriers to social inclusion as perceived by people with intellectual disabilities. *J. Intellect. Disabil.* **2006**, *33*, 83–89. [CrossRef] [PubMed]

8. Bassette, L.A.; Taber-Doughty, T.; Gama, R.I.; Alberto, P.; Yakubova, G.; Cihak, D. The use of cell phones to address safety skills for students with a moderate ID in community-based settings. *Focus Autism Other Dev. Disabil.* **2018**, *33*, 100–110. [CrossRef]
9. Emerson, E.; Hatton, C.; Robertson, J.; & Baines, S. Perceptions of neighbourhood quality, social and civic participation and the self rated health of British adults with intellectual disability: Cross sectional study. *BMC Public Health* **2014**, *14*, 1252. [CrossRef]
10. Fraser-Barbour, E.F.; Crocker, R.; Walker, R. Barriers and facilitators in supporting people with intellectual disability to report sexual violence: Perspectives of Australian disability and mainstream support providers. *J. Adult Prot.* **2018**, *20*, 5–16. [CrossRef]
11. Heiman, T.; Shemesh, D.O. Predictors of cyber-victimization of higher-education students with and without learning disabilities. *J. Youth Stud.* **2019**, *22*, 205–222. [CrossRef]
12. Kelley, K.R.; Test, D.W.; Cooke, N.L. Effects of picture prompts delivered by a video iPod on pedestrian navigation. *Except. Child.* **2013**, *79*, 459–474. [CrossRef]
13. Spooner, F.; Stern, B.; Test, D.W. Teaching first aid skills to adolescents who are moderately mentally handicapped. *Educ. Train. Mental Retard.* **1989**, *24*, 341–351.
14. Mechling, L.C.; O'Brien, E. Computer-based video instruction to teach students with intellectual disabilities to use public bus transportation. *Educ. Train. Autism Dev. Disabil.* **2010**, *45*, 230–241.
15. Mechling, L.C.; Seid, N.H. Use of handheld personal digital assistant (PDA) to self-prompt pedestrian travel by young adults with moderate intellectual disabilities. *Educ. Train. Autism Dev. Disabil.* **2011**, *46*, 220–223.
16. Thurman, T.R.; Snider, L.A.; Boris, N.W.; Kalisa, A.; Nyirazinyoye, L.; Brown, L. Barriers to the community support of orphans and vulnerable youth in Rwanda. *Soc. Sci. Med.* **2008**, *66*, 1557–1567. [CrossRef] [PubMed]
17. Demi, A.S.; Warren, N.A. Issues in conducting research with vulnerable families. *West. J. Nurs Res.* **1995**, *17*, 188–202. [CrossRef]
18. Scottish Government. *A Connected Scotland: Our Strategy for Tackling Social Isolation and Loneliness and Building Stronger Social Communities*; Scottish Government: Edinburgh, UK, 2018.
19. Myers, F.; Ager, A.; Kerr, P.; Myles, S. Outside looking in? Studies of the community integration of people with learning disabilities. *Disabil. Soc.* **1998**, *13*, 389–413. [CrossRef]
20. Hall, E. The entangled geographies of social exclusion/inclusion for people with learning disabilities. *Health Place* **2005**, *11*, 107–115. [CrossRef]
21. Hodges, Z.; Northway, R. Exploring professional decision making in relation to safeguarding: A grounded theory study of social workers and community nurses in community learning (intellectual) disability teams in Wales. *J. Appl. Res. Intellect. Disabil.* **2019**, *32*, 435–445. [CrossRef]
22. McCarthy, M.; Bates, C.; Triantafyllopoulou, P.; Hunt, S.; Skillman, K.M. "Put bluntly, they are targeted by the worst creeps society has to offer": Police and professionals' views and actions relating to domestic violence and women with intellectual disabilities. *J. Appl. Res. Intellect. Disabil.* **2017**, *32*, 71–81. [CrossRef]
23. Amado, A.N.; Stancliffe, R.J.; McCarron, M.; McCallion, P. Social inclusion and community participation of individuals with intellectual/developmental disabilities. *Intellect. Dev. Disabil.* **2013**, *51*, 360–375. [CrossRef]
24. Craig, D.; Bigby, C. "She's been involved in everything as far as I can see": Supporting the active participation of people with intellectual disability in community groups. *J. Intellect. Dev. Disabil.* **2015**, *40*, 12–25. [CrossRef]
25. Moyle, W.; Kellett, U.; Ballantyne, A.; Gracia, N. Dementia and loneliness: An Australian perspective. *J. Clin. Nurs.* **2011**, *20*, 1445–1453. [CrossRef] [PubMed]
26. Bowes, A.; Dawson, A.; Jepson, R.; McCabe, L. Physical activity for people with dementia: a scoping study. *BMC Geriatr.* **2013**, *13*, 129. [CrossRef] [PubMed]
27. World Health Organisation. Available online: https://apps.who.int/iris/bitstream/handle/10665/75263/9789241564458_eng.pdf;jsessionid=827DA8FA0F17170EFD46D42FA37663CB?sequence=1 (accessed on 15 June 2019).
28. DEEP. Available online: http://dementiavoices.org.uk/wp-content/uploads/2013/11/DEEP-Guide-Writing-dementia-friendly-information.pdf (accessed on 15 June 2019).
29. Morgan, D.G.; Semchuk, K.M.; Stewart, N.J.; D'Arcy, C. Job strain among staff of rural nursing homes. A comparison of nurses, aides, and activity workers. *J. Nurs. Adm.* **2002**, *32*, 152–161. [CrossRef] [PubMed]

30. Snyder, L.; Quayhagen, M.P.; Shepherd, S.; Bower, D. Supportive seminar groups: An intervention for early stage dementia patients. *Gerontologist* **1995**, *35*, 691–695. [CrossRef]
31. Roest, H.G.; Meiland, F.J.; Maroccini, R.; Comijs, H.C.; Jonker, C.; Dröes, R.M. Subjective needs of people with dementia: A review of the literature. *Int. Psychogeriatr.* **2007**, *19*, 559–592. [CrossRef]
32. Arthur, A.R. The emotional lives of people with learning disability. *Br. J. Learn. Disabil.* **2003**, *31*, 25–30. [CrossRef]
33. Brooker, D. What is person-centred care in dementia? *Rev. Clin. Gerontol.* **2004**, *13*, 215–222. [CrossRef]
34. Gould, S.; Dodd, K. 'Normal people can have a child but disability can't': The experiences of mothers with mild learning disabilities who have had their children removed. *Br. J. Learn. Disabil.* **2013**, *42*, 25–35. [CrossRef]
35. Gove, D.; Small, N.; Downs, M.; Vernooij-Dassen, M. General practitioners' perceptions of the stigma of dementia and the role of reciprocity. *Dementia* **2017**, *16*, 948–964.
36. Dementia Friendly Hospitals from a Universal Design Approach: Design Guidelines. Available online: http://dementia.ie/images/uploads/site-images/UD-DFH-Guidelines-2018-Full-doc-lw-res-compressed-A1.pdf (accessed on 19 May 2019).
37. Scottish Government. *The Keys to Life: Unlocking Futures for People with Learning Disabilities—Implementation Framework and Priorities 2019–2021*; Scottish Government: Edinburgh, UK, 2019.
38. World Health Organization. *Global Action Plan on the Public Health Response to Dementia 2017–2025*; World Health Organization: Geneva, Switzerland, 2017.
39. Braun, V.; Clarke, V. Using thematic analysis in psychology. *Qual. Res. Psychol.* **2006**, *3*, 77–101. [CrossRef]
40. Melunsky, N.; Crellin, N.; Dudzinski, E.; Orrell, M.; Wenborn, J.; Poland, F.; Woods, B.; Charlesworth, G. The experience of family carers attending a joint reminiscence group with people with dementia: A thematic analysis. *Dementia* **2015**, *14*, 842–859. [CrossRef] [PubMed]
41. Knox, M.; Mok, M.; Parmenter, T.R. Working with the experts: Collaborative research with people with an intellectual disability. *Disabil. Soc.* **2000**, *15*, 49–61. [CrossRef]
42. Goffman, E. *Stigma: Notes on the Management of Spoiled Identity*; Prentice-Hall: Englewood Cliffs, NJ, USA, 1963.
43. Dewees, M.; Pulice, R.T.; McCormick, L.L. Community integration of former state hospital patients: Outcomes of a policy shift in Vermont. *Psychiatr. Serv.* **1996**, *47*, 1088–1092.
44. Hogan, A.; McLellan, L.; Bauman, A. Health promotion needs of young people with disabilities—A population study. *Disabil. Rehabil.* **2000**, *22*, 352–357.
45. Heward, M.; Innes, A.; Cutler, C.; Hambridge, S. Dementia-friendly communities: Challenges and strategies for achieving stakeholder involvement. *Health Soc. Care* **2017**, *25*, 858–867. [CrossRef]
46. Lin, S. 'Dementia-friendly communities' and being dementia friendly in healthcare settings. *Curr. Opin. Psychiatry* **2017**, *30*, 145–150. [CrossRef]
47. Lin, S.; Lewis, F.M. Dementia friendly, dementia capable, and dementia positive: Concepts to prepare for the future. *Gerontologist* **2015**, *55*, 237–244. [CrossRef]
48. Swaffer, K. Dementia: Stigma, language, and dementia-friendly. *Dementia* **2014**, *13*, 709–716. [CrossRef]
49. Alzheimer Scotland. Available online: https://www.alzscot.org/dementia_friendly_communities (accessed on 30 April 2019).
50. Botsford, J.; Dening, K.H. Working positively with culture, ethnicity and dementia. In *Dementia, Culture and Ethnicity: Issues for All*; Botsford, J., Dening, K.H., Eds.; Jessica Kingsley Publishers: London, UK, 2015.
51. Roulstone, A.; Thomas, P.; Balderston, S. Between hate and vulnerability: Unpacking the British criminal justice system's construction of disablist hate crime. *Disabil. Soc.* **2011**, *26*, 351–364. [CrossRef]
52. Doherty, G. Do mates hate? A framing of the theoretical position of mate crime and an assessment of its practical impact. *J. Adult Prot.* **2015**, *17*, 296–307. [CrossRef]
53. Thomas, P. 'Mate crime': Ridicule, hostility and targeted attacks against disabled people. *Disabil. Soc.* **2011**, *26*, 107–111. [CrossRef]
54. Hollomotz, A. 'A lad tried to get hold of my boobs, so I kicked him': An examination of attempts by adults with learning difficulties to initiate their own safeguarding. *Disabil. Soc.* **2012**, *27*, 117–129. [CrossRef]
55. Joyce, T.A. An audit of investigations into allegations of abuse involving adults with intellectual disability. *J. Intellect. Disabil. Res.* **2003**, *47*, 606–616. [CrossRef] [PubMed]
56. Macdonald, S.J. 'Community fear and harassment': learning difficulties and hate crime incidents in the north-east of England. *Disability Soc.* **2015**, *30*, 353–367. [CrossRef]

57. Grundy, D. Friend or fake? Mate crimes and people with learning disabilities. *J. Intellect. Disabil. Offending Behav.* **2011**, *2*, 167–169. [CrossRef]
58. Safety Net. Available online: https://arcuk.org.uk/safetynet/project-background/ (accessed on 15 May 2019).
59. O'Rourke, A.; Grey, I.M.; Fuller, R.; McClean, B. Satisfaction with living arrangements of older adults with intellectual disability, service users' and carers' views. *J. Intellect. Disabil.* **2004**, *8*, 12–29.
60. Kenny, A.; Power, M. Social inclusion and intellectual disability in Ireland: Social inclusion co-ordinators' perspectives on barriers and opportunities. *Scott. J. Resid. Child. Care* **2018**, *17*, 4.
61. Smith, R.W. Leisure of disabled tourists; barriers to participation. *Ann. Tour. Res.* **1987**, *14*, 376–389. [CrossRef]
62. Gladwell, N.J.; Bedini, L.A. In search of lost leisure: The impact of caregiving on leisure travel. *Tour. Manag.* **2004**, *25*, 685–693. [CrossRef]
63. Hall, S.A. Community involvement of young adults with intellectual disabilities: Their experiences and perspectives on inclusion. *J. Appl. Res. Intellect. Disabil.* **2017**, *30*, 859–871. [CrossRef] [PubMed]
64. Scottish Commission for Learning Disability. Available online: https://www.scld.org.uk/wp-content/uploads/2017/01/Final-report-web-version.pdf (accessed on 22 May 2019).
65. Deal, M. Disabled people's attitudes toward other impairment groups: A hierarchy of impairments. *Disabil. Soc.* **2003**, *18*, 897–910. [CrossRef]
66. Salmon, N. 'We just stick together': How disabled teens negotiate stigma to create lasting friendship. *J. Intellect. Disabil. Res.* **2013**, *57*, 347–358. [CrossRef] [PubMed]
67. Gerber, P.J. The impact of learning disabilities on adulthood: A review of the evidence-based literature for research and practice in adult education. *J. Learn. Disabil.* **2012**, *45*, 31–46. [CrossRef] [PubMed]
68. Wiersma, E.C.; Denton, A. From social network to safety net: Dementia-friendly communities in rural northern Ontario. *Dementia* **2016**, *15*, 51–68. [CrossRef] [PubMed]
69. Alzheimer's Society. Available online: https://www.alzheimers.org.uk/get-involved/dementia-friendly-communities/what-dementia-friendly-community (accessed on 30 April 2019).
70. McGhee, G.; Atkinson, J. The carer/ key worker relationship cycle: A theory of the reciprocal process. *J. Psychiatr. Ment. Health Nurs.* **2010**, *17*, 312–318. [CrossRef]
71. Parkinson, M.; Carr, S.M.; Rushmer, R.; Abley, C. Investigating what works to support family carers of people with dementia: A rapid realist review. *J. Public Health* **2016**, *39*, e290–e301. [CrossRef]
72. Shalock, R.L.; Verdugo, M.A.; Jenaro, C.; Wang, M.; Wehmeyer, M.; Jiancheng, X.; Lachapelle, Y. Cross-cultural study of quality of life indicators. *Am. J. Ment. Retard.* **2005**, *110*, 298–311. [CrossRef]
73. HM Government. 2018. Available online: https://assets.publishing.service.gov.uk/government/uploads/system/uploads/attachment_data/file/750909/6.4882_DCMS_Loneliness_Strategy_web_Update.pdf (accessed on 4 June 2019).
74. Beart, S.; Hawkins, D.; Kroese, B.S.; Smithson, P.; Tolosa, I. Barriers to accessing leisure opportunities for people with learning disabilities. *Br. J. Learn. Disabil.* **2001**, *29*, 133–138. [CrossRef]
75. Carmien, S.; Dawe, M.; Fischer, G.; Gorman, A.; Kintsch, A.; Sullivan, J.F., Jr. Socio-technical environments supporting people with cognitive disabilities using public transportation. *ACM Trans. Comput. Human Interact.* **2005**, *12*, 233–262. [CrossRef]
76. Keep Safe. Available online: http://www.iammescotland.co.uk/keep-safe/ (accessed on 15 May 2019).
77. Bees, S. Some aspects of the friendship networks of people with learning difficulties. *Clin. Psychol. Forum* **1991**, *31*, 12–14.
78. Rowe, M.A.; Vandeveer, S.S.; Greenblum, C.A.; List, C.N.; Fernandez, R.M.; Mixson, N.; Ahn, H.C. Persons with dementia missing in the community: Is it wandering or something unique? *BMC Geriatr.* **2011**, *11*. [CrossRef] [PubMed]
79. I Am Me. Available online: http://www.iammescotland.co.uk/keep-safe/about-keep-safe/ (accessed on 30 April 2019).
80. Power, A.; Bartlett, R. Self-building safe havens in a post-service landscape: How adults with learning disabilities are reclaiming the welcoming communities agenda. *Soc. Cult. Geogr.* **2018**, *19*, 336–356. [CrossRef]
81. Knafo-Noam, A.; Uzefovsky, F.; Israel, S.; Davidov, M.; Zahn-Waxler, C. The prosocial personality and its facets: Genetic and environmental architecture of mother-reported behaviour of 7-year old twins. *Front. Psychol.* **2015**, *6*, 1–9. [CrossRef] [PubMed]

82. Canter, D.; Youngs, D.; Yaneva, M. Towards a measure of kindness: An exploration of a neglected interpersonal trait. *Personal. Individ. Differ.* **2017**, *106*, 15–20. [CrossRef]
83. Cutler, J.; Campbell-Meiklejohn, D. A comparative fMRI meta-analysis of altruistic and strategic decisions to give. *NeuroImage* **2019**, *184*, 227–241. [CrossRef]
84. Unwin, J. Kindness, emotions and human relationships: the blind spot in public policy. Carnegie UK Trust: Dunfermline, UK, 2018.
85. Dewar, B.; Nolan, M. Caring about caring: Developing a model to implement compassionate relationship centred care in an older people care setting. *Int. J. Nurs. Stud.* **2013**, *50*, 1247–1258. [CrossRef]
86. Stephen, G. Compassionate care enhancement: Benefits and outcomes. *Int. J. Pers. Cent. Med.* **2011**, *1*, 808–813.
87. Department of Health. *Compassion in Practice: Nursing, Midwifery and Care Staff. Our Vision and Strategy*; The Stationery Office: London, UK, 2012.
88. SMCI Associates and Prescott Clements Associates. *Compassionate Connections Workforce Development Programme to Support Implementation of the Refreshed Framework for Maternity Care in Scotland Evaluation Report to NHS Education for Scotland*; NHS Education Scotland: Edinburgh, UK, 2014.
89. Barrie, K.; Miller, E.; O'Brien, M. *Compassionate Inverclyde: Evaluation Summary Report*; IFIC: Oxford, UK, 2018.
90. Ferguson, Z. The Place of Kindness: Combating Loneliness and Building Stronger Communities. Carnegie UK Trust: Dunfermline, UK, 2017.
91. Commission for Architecture and the Built Environment. Available online: https://www.designcouncil.org.uk/sites/default/files/asset/document/the-principles-of-inclusive-design.pdf (accessed on 5 June 2019).
92. Bigby, C.; Anderson, S.; Cameron, N. Identifying conceptualizations and theories of change embedded in interventions to facilitate community participation for people with intellectual disability: A scoping review. *J. Appl. Res. Intellect. Disabil.* **2018**, *31*, 165–180. [CrossRef]
93. Stewart, K.; Bradshaw, J.; Beadle-Brown, J. Evaluating service users' experiences using Talking Mats®. *Tizard Learn. Disabil. Rev.* **2018**, *23*, 78–86. [CrossRef]
94. Overmars-Marx, T.; Thomése, F.; Meininger, H. Neighbourhood social inclusion from the perspective of people with intellectual disabilities: Relevant themes identified with the use of photovoice. *J. Appl. Res. Intellectual Disabilities* **2019**, *32*, 82–93. [CrossRef] [PubMed]
95. Fenn, K.; Scior, K. The psychological and social impact of self-advocacy group membership on people with intellectual disabilities: A literature review. *J. Appl. Res. Intellectual Disabilities* **2019**, *32*, 1349–1358. [CrossRef] [PubMed]
96. Ashley, D.; Fossey, E.; Bigby, C. The home environments and occupational engagement of people with intellectual disabilities in supported living. *British J. Occup. Ther.* **2019**, *11*, 698–709l. [CrossRef]

© 2019 by the authors. Licensee MDPI, Basel, Switzerland. This article is an open access article distributed under the terms and conditions of the Creative Commons Attribution (CC BY) license (http://creativecommons.org/licenses/by/4.0/).

Article

Safety Culture among Private and Professional Drivers in Norway and Greece: Examining the Influence of National Road Safety Culture

Tor-Olav Nævestad [1,*], Alexandra Laiou [2], Ross O. Phillips [1], Torkel Bjørnskau [1] and George Yannis [2]

1. Institute of Transport Economics, Gaustadalleen 21, 0349 Oslo, Norway; rph@toi.no (R.O.P.); tbj@toi.no (T.B.)
2. National Technical University of Athens, Zografou Campus, Iroon Polytechniou 5, GR-15773 Athens, Greece; alaiou@central.ntua.gr (A.L.); geyannis@central.ntua.gr (G.Y.)
* Correspondence: ton@toi.no

Received: 1 February 2019; Accepted: 2 April 2019; Published: 16 April 2019

Abstract: While Norway had the lowest road mortality rate in Europe in 2017, Greece had one of the worst road safety records of all EU-27 countries. The present study investigates road safety culture (RSC) as an explanation for this discrepancy by: (1) Comparing the road safety behaviours among professional and private drivers in Norway and Greece, (2) Examining factors influencing road safety behaviours, focusing especially on national road safety culture, and (3) Examining the influence of road safety behaviours and other factors (e.g., demographic and work-related variables) on accident involvement. This is done by comparing survey answers of private car (N = 796) and professional drivers (heavy goods vehicles and buses) in Norway and Greece (N = 416). Results from qualitative interviews (N = 61) are also presented. We study safety behaviours hypothesized to vary according to nationality (e.g., aggressive violations), and behaviours hypothesized to vary according to the professional versus private driver dimension (e.g., seat belt use). A central objective is to examine whether the former safety behaviours are more similar among private and professional drivers within countries than among professional and private drivers across national samples, indicating common national road safety cultures among private and professional drivers in the respective countries. The results indicate that aggressive violations are more similar among private and professional drivers within the national samples, than across the national samples, while seat belt use seems to vary according to the professional versus private dimension. The results also indicate a relationship between aggressive violations and accident involvement, although other variables were more strongly correlated. Moreover, drivers' safety behaviours were influenced by the behaviours that these groups ascribed to other drivers in their countries, indicating the existence of different national road safety cultures. The Greek RSC was characterized by more aggression and violations than the Norwegian RSC, which seemed to be characterized by a higher level of compliance and politeness. The different RSCs may perhaps shed light on the different accident records in the two countries.

Keywords: safety culture; safety behaviours; private and professional drivers; Norway; Greece

1. Introduction

1.1. Background and Aims

Road traffic crashes are a major cause of death among all age groups. About 1.35 million people are killed annually on the world's roads, while between 20 and 50 million people are non-fatally injured [1]. The numbers of people killed or severely injured in road crashes have gradually been reduced in recent years, as a result of traditional safety strategies focusing on safety behaviours, technology, and infrastructure [2]. There are, however, still possibilities for further reductions, but it has been argued that this requires the application of new approaches to road safety. The safety culture perspective comprises such a new approach, with a great potential to reduce road accidents, as culture makes up an important risk factor not currently addressed by traditional interventions [3–5].

The relationship between organizational safety culture/climate and safety outcomes is well-documented in meta analyses of organizational safety [6,7]. Previous studies indicate a high focus on organizational safety culture in other transport sectors with a recognized high safety level, especially aviation [8,9], but also the maritime sector [10] and rail [11]. Explaining the safety performance in these sectors, these studies point to safety culture as an indispensable factor [8–11]. The safety culture level of aviation is, for instance, used as a model for improving safety culture in oil and gas [8], and also in other industries and sectors. Accordingly, studies report relatively successful implementations of safety management systems (SMSs) aiming to facilitate the development of a positive safety culture in rail [11] and in the maritime sector [10]. In comparison, it seems that the safety culture perspective has been applied to some extent by companies and regulators in the road sector. This is partly due to the fact that the road sector lacks SMS requirements focusing on safety culture. Studies have nevertheless found strong relationships between organizational safety culture and safety outcomes in the road sector (e.g., [12–15]).

The concepts of safety culture and climate have traditionally been applied to organizations. Organizational safety culture can be defined as shared and safety-relevant ways of thinking or acting that are (re)created through the joint negotiation of people in social settings [16]. Safety climate can be conceived of as "snapshots", or manifestations of safety culture [17]. As drivers at work are members of organizations, they have been subjected to organizational safety culture/climate studies, which have documented a relationship between culture/climate and safety outcomes (e.g., behaviours, near misses, accidents) [12,14,15]. About 40% of fatal accidents in Norway involve drivers at work [18]. Most of these are members of organizations, and thus susceptible to organizational safety culture measures.

The safety culture perspective has, however, only recently been applied to the road sector, and more research is needed if we are to exploit its full potential as a tool for developing road safety measures. An important step in this process is to also employ the safety culture concept to analytical units additional to organizations [4,5]. Edwards et al. [5] conclude that road safety culture (RSC) can be understood as a different application of the same foundational concept as organizational safety culture. The difference is that when we apply the safety culture to road safety in general, we also apply it to other sociocultural units than organizations. This involves also applying it to private car drivers, and the sociocultural units that they are part of, e.g., nations, communities, and peer groups [4,5]. As Luria et al. [19] suggest, most drivers on the road at any one time are not at work. Given the potential importance of the safety culture perspective for road safety, we should therefore also employ it to private drivers, especially since these include groups (e.g., young and old drivers) with higher accident risk. There are, however, few studies applying the road safety culture/climate concept to private drivers [3,5,19]. Those that do exist concur that the safety culture concept should not necessarily be restricted to organizations, but applied to other social units, such as nations, regions, sectors, communities, and peer groups (cf. [3,5,19]). This is a relatively unresearched issue that the present study contributes to.

Differences in national road fatality rates indicate that the national level is a key sociocultural unit to also apply the safety culture perspective to, and it is not unreasonable to hypothesize that differences between national RSC may shed light on national differences in fatality rates (cf. [3]). Studies of national differences between road safety behaviours (e.g., [20,21]) often hypothesize that the results indicate differences in national culture, without specifying or measuring the (cultural) mechanisms generating these different national behaviours. Several factors that could influence road safety culture are national (e.g., traffic rules, the police enforcing the rules, road user interaction, infrastructure). For these reasons, we could expect the existence of different national road safety cultures. On the other hand, we could perhaps hypothesize that some groups within countries, e.g., professional drivers, are less influenced by national RSC, as they undergo EU-standardized training (Directive 2003/59/EC), and as they often are members of organizations that are obliged to facilitate to safe transport. Professional drivers differ from private drivers in several important respects. First, professional drivers, unless they are self-employed, drive as part of an employment relationship, and they are members of work organizations. Previous studies have found that managers' focus on safety issues and organizational safety culture influence professional drivers' safety behaviours [12–14]. Organizational safety culture may reduce the (negative) impact of national safety culture [22]. Second, professional drivers often relate to deadlines and customers, and previous studies have found that their perceived levels of time pressure and stress influence their road safety behaviour [12,13]. We expand more on these issues below. By comparing different groups (private and professional drivers) within the same countries, we will be able to examine the importance of national road safety culture for road safety behaviours and accident involvement. If certain road safety behaviours vary less among driver groups within than across the national samples, we may hypothesize that this could be due to the influence of national RSC.

An empirical study was therefore conducted, aiming to: (1) Compare the road safety behaviours among professional and private drivers in Norway and Greece, (2) Examine the factors influencing road safety behaviours, focusing especially on national road safety culture, and (3) Examine the influence of road safety behaviours and other factors (e.g., demographic and work-related variables) on accident involvement. The present paper compares private car and professional drivers (heavy goods vehicles and buses) in Norway and Greece. We study safety behaviours that are hypothesized to vary according to nationality (e.g., aggressive violations), and behaviours that are hypothesized to vary according to the professional versus private driver dimension (e.g., seat belt use). A central objective of the study is to examine whether the former safety behaviours are more similar among private and professional drivers within the countries than among professional and private drivers across national samples, indicating common national road safety cultures among private and professional drivers in the respective countries. In the present study, we define road safety culture (RSC) as shared patterns of behaviour, shared norms prescribing certain road safety behaviours and thus shared expectations regarding the behaviours of others.

Norway and Greece were selected for comparison since the road safety status in the two countries differs significantly. Norway had the lowest road mortality rate in Europe with 20 road deaths per million inhabitants in 2017, and the lowest road death risk [23]. In comparison, the mortality rate in Greece in 2017 was 69 road deaths per million inhabitants, which was well above the EU average of 50 [23]. According to Yannis and Papadimitriou [24], Greece has one of the worst road safety records of all EU-27 countries. The fatality rate of Greece was higher than the EU average in all years between 2001 and 2014. The age-standardized number of deaths for all forms of road transport in 2010 was 136 per million population, with only Romania performing worse [25]. The corresponding figure for Norway in 2010 was 52 per million citizens. Greek motorists also report poorer safety behaviours in traffic, and recent research points to serious flaws in the way road safety is managed at all levels in Greece [26,27].

Our study is carried out as part of a research project titled "Safety culture in private and professional transport: examining its influence on behaviours and implications for interventions", funded by the Norwegian Research Council and undertaken by the Institute of Transport Economics (TØI, Norway) and the National Technical University of Athens (NTUA, Greece). Results from this project focusing only on professional drivers have been presented in conference papers, focusing on heavy goods vehicle (HGV) drivers [28] and bus drivers [29]. The conference paper on bus drivers was also developed into a journal paper [22]. The present study builds on these previous studies by including and comparing findings from private drivers from Norway and Greece. A very short and previous version of the present study has also been presented as a conference paper [30]. The results in the present study have also been presented in an extended Norwegian Safe Culture project report, which also presents full results from 61 qualitative interviews [31].

1.2. Previous Research

1.2.1. Factors Influencing Safety Behaviours among Private and Professional Drivers

The present paper compares factors influencing safety behaviours among professional and private drivers. Road safety behaviours are measured by means of the driver behavior questionnaire (DBQ). The DBQ originally distinguished between three types of aberrant behaviours, based on Reason et al. [32]: lapses, errors, and violations. Lapses typically involve problems with attention and memory. Errors typically involve observation failures and misjudgments. Violations involve deliberate deviations from safe driving practices (cf. [33]).

Age, Gender, Experience. Previous research has found that demographic variables (e.g., age, gender, nationality) influence the road safety behaviour of both private and professional drivers. Research on private drivers finds that older drivers and females are more inclined to be involved in lapses, while errors do not seem to be related to any specific demographic groups [34]. Moreover, violations (which seem to be the behaviour most strongly related to accidents) seem to be more prevalent among young drivers and male drivers [34]. Previous research on private drivers has also established a relationship between drivers' level of education and driving behaviours. In a study using the DBQ in a Czech population of drivers, Sucha et al. [35] report, for instance, lower levels of what they term dangerous violations and dangerous errors with increasing levels of education.

Organisational and Work-Related Variables. As indicated above, previous studies have found relationships between organizational safety culture/climate and DBQ items [12–14] for professional drivers, and also between time pressure, stress, and DBQ items [12,13]. Davey et al. [12] suggest that higher perceived levels of work/pressure stress are related to mistakes for professional drivers, while Öz et al. [13] find that higher perceived levels of work/pressure stress are related to errors and violations.

Nationality. Previous research has highlighted nationality as a risk factor, indicating that being foreign to the road infrastructure may influence both behaviour and accident risk [36]. To understand the emerging issue of young drivers' involvement in traffic accidents abroad, Huang et al. [37] compared risk-taking behaviors in familiar and unfamiliar driving situations. Results showed that risk-taking behaviors while driving in unfamiliar conditions were mediated by psychological factors, such as self-assessment of being a good driver, more than the actual knowledge of road regulation rules. There are some cross-cultural studies of safety behaviours using DBQ items among private drivers (e.g., [20,21]). Warner et al. [21] compare safety behaviours among private drivers in Finland, Sweden, Turkey, and Greece (each with N = 200). The study identifies nine key DBQ items that drivers from different countries rate differently. Warner et al. [21] found a higher prevalence of aggressive violations (e.g., become angered and indicate hostility, sound the horn to indicate annoyance) and ordinary violations (pull too far out of a junction) in Greece and Turkey than in Sweden and Finland. They also found a higher prevalence of over speeding in Sweden and Finland than the two other countries. Finally, they found a higher prevalence of lapses in Finland than the other countries. Özkan et al. [20] compare DBQ items in six countries: Finland, Great Britain, Greece, Iran, The Netherlands, and Turkey (each with N = 240). One of the main results from this study is that that Greek drivers reported to commit aggressive violations more often than other nationalities, especially behaviours indicating their annoyance and hostility to other road users. Drivers from Western/Northern European countries, on the other hand, scored higher on ordinary violations, especially on the "speeding on a motorway" item.

It is important to note that only some road safety behaviours (DBQ items) can be related to national road safety culture, and that variation in road safety behaviours also should be sought by looking at other variables. Consequently, we have included two variables in the study that we primarily expect to vary according to the professional versus private dimension. These items are: driving under the influence of alcohol and driving without using a seatbelt. The first is a crucial predictor of accident involvement, while the latter is strongly related to the severity of accidents [2]. The prevalence of driving while under the influence of alcohol is lower for professional drivers than it is for drivers of private cars, although this also varies between countries [38]. Additionally, professional drivers are less inclined to wear a seat belt than private drivers, although this has improved in recent years [39].

1.2.2. Factors Influencing Accident Involvement among Private and Professional Drivers

Demographic Variables. Nationality is a crucial demographic variable influencing the accident risk of both professional drivers of heavy vehicles and private drivers of passenger vehicles [26,36,40]. Moreover, age is also an important variable influencing accident risk for both professional and private drivers [41,42]. The same applies to gender: male drivers have a higher risk of being involved in accidents with passenger cars than female drivers [42]. Focusing on private drivers, Özkan et al. [43] study how sex (male and female) and gender roles (masculinity and femininity) and their interaction were associated with driving skills and accident involvement among young drivers. Sex (male) predicted accidents, while masculinity predicted positively perceptual-motor skills, and femininity predicted positively the safety skills.

Safety Behaviours. In a meta study of 174 studies using the DBQs and measures of self-reported accidents, De Winter and Dodou [44] found especially violations, but also errors, predicted accidents. Moreover, in their study of safety behaviours among private drivers in Finland, Sweden, Turkey, and Greece, Warner et al. [21] found that five of the DBQ items predicted driver self-reported accident involvement (for the last three years) in an analysis where all the countries were taken together.

Mileage. The number of kilometers driven each year is an important risk factor influencing the risk of being involved in an accident. Although the number of accidents per kilometer may be fairly similar for professional and private drivers [2], professional drivers are statistically more likely to have experienced an accident each year than private drivers, as professionals drive more kilometers each year.

Time pressure and stress. Time pressure and stress may influence the accident risk of professional drivers [18]. This relationship often seems to be mediated by safety behaviour [12,13].

Sector (focus on safety). For professional drivers, sector or subsector may also influence accident risk. HGVs transporting dangerous goods have a 75% lower accident risk than other HGVs [2], presumably as the sector focus on safety is higher, as indicated by rules/enforcement, training, and transport buyers' focus on safety.

1.3. *What Is National Road Safety Culture?*

Edwards et al. [5] note that, although the concept of "driving culture" was already introduced in 1992, there are still no definitions of road safety culture that are commonly accepted by road safety researchers. Edwards et al. [5] review the status of the road safety culture concept, in a paper contributing to a 2014 special issue (in "Transportation Research Part F") devoted to traffic safety culture. Their review concludes that most of the current literature on the concept was collected in an anthology collecting papers from the American Automobile Association's (AAA) workshop on road safety culture [45]. The definitions of road safety culture provided by the contributors to the anthology were, e.g., the "beliefs, norms and values and things people use that guide their social interactions in everyday life" [46], "implicit shared values and beliefs", and "common practices, expectations and informal rules that drivers learn by observation from others in their communities" [47]. These aspects of RSC can be studied both by using quantitative and qualitative methods. Among the few studies available of RSC, the quantitative approach is the most common, measuring RSC by means of safety climate questionnaires (e.g., [19,48–50]). RSC can, however, also be studied by means of in-depth qualitative studies (e.g., ethnography, interviews), elucidating deeper patterns of meaning motivating and legitimizing behaviours, and which are related to identity (e.g., [51]).

The mentioned studies of national differences between DBQ items [20,21] often hypothesize that the results indicate differences in national culture. These studies do not, however, directly measure RSC or specify the (cultural) mechanisms generating these different national behaviours. According to

Ward et al. [3], research on road safety culture often seems to lack an explanation of the theoretical link between safety culture and safety behaviours. They state that the applicability of the safety culture perspective requires the development of a theoretical model to explain this relationship.

In the present study, we define RSC as shared patterns of behaviour, shared norms prescribing certain road safety behaviours, and thus shared expectations regarding the behaviours of others. Road safety culture can be understood as a different application of the same foundational concept as organizational safety culture [5], which generally is defined as shared and safety-relevant ways of thinking and acting [16]. Thus, our definition of road safety culture seems to include the most important aspects, focusing on shared patterns of behaviour, shared norms, and shared expectations. Other studies have, however, also included shared values, beliefs, assumptions, etc. The latter aspects of RSC (shared norms and expectations) are operationalized as descriptive norms, which refer to individuals' perceptions of what other people actually do [52]. Descriptive norms may influence behaviour by providing information about what is normal [52]. Operationalizing RSC partly as descriptive norms, we may refer to the mechanism mediating between safety culture (shared norms and expectations) and safety behaviours as "subtle social pressures" [52]. It is also important to note that descriptive norms can also influence behaviour through the false consensus bias, in which individuals overestimate the prevalence of risky behaviour among their peers in order to justify their own behavior [53].

Finally, as discussed by Nævestad and Bjørnskau [4] and Edwards et al. [5], safety culture is a concept that can be related to several different sociocultural units. Although studies of professional drivers indicate the importance of organizational safety culture [12,14], other studies indicate the importance of regional road safety culture [49], community safety climate [19], and RSC related to peer-groups [50].

1.4. Hypotheses

Based on previous research, we first hypothesize that there will be more aggressive violations in the Greek sample than in the Norwegian sample (Hypothesis 1). Second, we assume that there will be more over speeding in the Norwegian sample than in the Greek sample (Hypothesis 2). Third, we hypothesize that some safety behaviours (i.e., aggressive violations and over speeding) will be more similar among private and professional drivers within the national samples, than among professional and private drivers across the national samples (Hypothesis 3), indicating different national RSC (specified as shared patterns of behaviour) in the two countries. Fourth, in accordance with previous research, we hypothesize that other safety behaviours (i.e., driving under the influence and seat belt use) will be more similar between private drivers and professional drivers across countries, indicating that being a private or professional driver is more important than nationality in these instances (Hypothesis 4). Fifth, we also measure national RSC as descriptive norms, and hypothesize that we will see relatively similar scores comparing means for national RSC between the groups within countries, but significantly different when comparing groups across countries (Hypothesis 5). In accordance with this, we expect relationships between respondents' behaviours and national RSC, especially on the variables that we primarily hypothesize to vary according to nationality. Sixth, we hypothesize that the safety behaviours of professional drivers will be influenced by work-related variables, such as organizational safety culture, time pressure, and sector focus on safety (Hypothesis 6). Seventh, we hypothesize that the safety behaviours of private drivers will be influenced by factors such as the road safety culture in their community, or in their peer groups, and their level of education (Hypothesis 7). Eight, we hypothesize that professional and private car drivers' safety behaviours will be influenced by demographic variables, such as age, gender, and nationality (Hypothesis 8). Ninth, we hypothesize that drivers' accident involvement will be influenced by their safety behaviours (e.g., aggressive violations) (Hypothesis 9). Tenth, we hypothesize that drivers' accident involvement will be influenced by demographic variables, such as age, gender, and nationality (Hypothesis 10). Eleventh, we hypothesize that drivers' accident involvement will be influenced by their mileage (Hypothesis

11). Twelfth, we hypothesize that work-related variables, such as time pressure and stress, sector, and framework conditions, will influence the accident risk of professional drivers (Hypothesis 12).

2. Methods

2.1. Recruitment of Respondents

The Norwegian professional driver respondents were recruited in the last trimester of 2016 through the Norwegian researchers' contact with Norwegian transport companies and unions. Web links to the questionnaires were distributed along with an introductory text explaining the purpose of the survey and stressing that the surveys were confidential. The Norwegian private driver respondents were recruited through the Preference Database of the Norwegian Postal Service, consisting of 430,000 people in 2016, who had consented to receive information or advertising through the moving or holiday service of the Postal Service. In September 2017, e-mails with web-links to the survey were submitted to 45,483 people in three Norwegian counties. Of the 45,452 people who received the e-mail, 6727 people (14.8%) opened the e-mail, and 645 (9.6%) completed the survey. Surveys were sent to three Norwegian counties, and one of these was the capital Oslo. Counties were selected based on differences in accident risk and attitudes. In an attempt to increase response rates, Norwegian respondents were informed that they could participate in a draw for a present card of 2000 NOK, if they wanted to. The Greek respondents (N = 416) were recruited through a marketing research company in Greece, which was under the scientific supervision of researchers from the NTUA. Recruitment of drivers in Greece was also difficult; therefore, it was decided to approach candidates in person and further explain the scope of the survey. This helped eliminate their doubts and fears about confidentiality, and the use of the information they would provide. The private drivers in Greece were sampled from two different areas: the capital Athens and the Greek island Rhodes. This sampling is based on an assumption that the RSC on an island could be different from the capital, as an island is a geographical enclosed area, and as it has many tourist drivers.

2.2. Survey Themes

Demographic variables. Both the survey to professional drivers and the survey to private drivers included questions on age, experience as a driver, gender, nationality, kilometers driven with a professional or private car in the last two years, etc. (cf. Hypothesis 8).

Questions to Private Drivers. For private drivers, questions were also included on their highest attained level of education, their place of living (e.g., rural, urban), for how long they have had their driver's license, how often they drive, the type of car they usually drive, etc. Private car drivers were also asked about the driving behavior of their closest friends who regularly drive a car. These questions were intended to measure peer road safety culture (cf. Hypothesis 7).

Questions to Professional Drivers. The survey to professional drivers included work-related variables with potential safety consequences, e.g., drivers' experiences with work and time pressure that may compromise safety, payment types (e.g., bonus for efficiency), management focus on driving style, and seat belt use. The professional driver survey also included an organizational culture index, consisting of 10 questions (cf. [22]) from the Global Aviation Information Network (GAIN) scale on organizational safety culture [54]. Professional drivers were also asked questions intended to measure sector focus on safety (cf. Hypothesis 6).

Safety Behaviours. The present study reports results of seven questions on road safety behaviour (cf. Hypotheses 1–4). Most of these were taken from the DBQ and based on the results of previous research [21]. Five of these were DBQ questions that Scandinavian and Southern European drivers have scored significantly different on in previous studies, and which were related to accident involvement [21] (cf. Table 5). The sixth item is related to driving under the influence of alcohol, which is one of the single factors that has been found to be one of the most important predictors of accident involvement [2]. The seventh item is "Drive without using a seat belt", as a seatbelt is a measure that may reduce the risk of being killed or severely injured with 60% for drivers of light vehicles and with between 47% and 42% for drivers of heavy vehicles, respectively [55]. Seat belt use is, however, related to the severity and not the occurrence of accidents. The DBQ answer alternatives have been changed from relative to absolute alternatives (e.g., Question: "For every ten trips, how often do you ... ?", Alternative answers: "Never", "Once or twice", "Three or four times", "Five or six times", "Seven or eight times", "More than eight times but not always", "Always"). Answer alternatives were changed, as previous research indicates that different demographic groups tend to interpret questions and formulations differently (i.e., what does "often" mean?) (cf. [56]).

National RSC Index. In addition to drawing inferences about national RSC based on national shared patterns of behaviour (among private and professional drivers), we also measure national RSC as descriptive norms [52], reflecting drivers' perceptions of what other drivers in our country do (cf. Hypothesis 5). The survey includes nine questions on expectations of other road users. Seven of these reflect those used for respondents' own behavior, while two questions concern compliance and politeness (Cf. Table 8). Five answer alternatives ranged between 1 (none-very few) and 5 (almost all/all).

Safety Outcomes. We report results for one question on respondents' crash involvement while driving (private or professionally) in the last two years, with four answer alternatives: (1) no, (2) yes involving property damage, (3) yes, involving personal injuries, (4) yes, involving fatal injuries (cf. Hypotheses 9–12).

2.3. Analysis of the Quantitative Data

Factor Analysis. We conduct factor analyses in the paper; one of the items measuring road safety behaviour, and one of the items measuring national RSC. In these analyses, we examine whether the studied items comprise a smaller number of coherent subscales, "factors", i.e., whether items load on underlying factors (e.g., aggressive behaviour in traffic). We employ either a confirmatory or an exploratory approach, depending on whether previous research indicates a given number of factors or not.

Cronbach's Alpha. We construct several indexes of different concepts (e.g., the factors) to compare how different groups score on these concepts. Cronbach's Alpha measures the correlation among responses on the indexes. The value varies between 0 and 1. A Cronbach's Alpha over 0.9 is very high, a score between 0.7 and 0.9 is good, a score between 0.5 and 0.6 is acceptable, and a score below 0.5 is unacceptable.

Comparison of Means. We also compare whether mean scores on the indexes are different, when testing, e.g., Hypotheses 1–4, in accordance with the first aim of our study, and Hypothesis 5, which is related to the second aim. When comparing the mean scores of different groups, we use one-way ANOVA tests, which compare whether the mean scores are equal (the null hypothesis) or (significantly) different. We also use two-way ANOVA, e.g., to test for interaction effects.

Regression Analyses. We conduct regression analyses when testing Hypotheses 6–12, in accordance with the second aim of our study. A total of 15 regression analyses are conducted. In the first 12 analyses, we use linear regression analysis, examining the factors predicting four different types of road safety behaviours. We conduct three analyses for each road safety behaviour variable: one for both professional and private drivers in Norway and Greece, one for only professional drivers in both countries, and one for only private car drivers in both countries. The separate analyses enable us to test the hypotheses on the unique factors influencing the safety behaviours of private (Hypotheses 7 and 8) and professional drivers (Hypotheses 6 and 8). The most basic independent variables are included first (e.g., gender, age, nationality), then the other independent variables are included.

Finally, we conduct four logistic regression analyses when testing Hypotheses 9–12, in accordance with the third aim of the study. In these analyses, we examine the factors predicting respondents' answers on the dependent variable measuring accident involvement. Logistic regression analysis is used in these analyses, as the dependent variable has two values (no = 1, yes = 2). B values are presented, and they indicate whether the risk of personal injuries is reduced (negative B values) or increased (positive B values), when the independent variables increase with one value. Of course, it is impossible to conclude about causality, as this is a cross-sectional and correlational study. The term 'predict' is nevertheless used when the regression analyses are described.

2.4. Qualitative Interviews

As noted, Nævestad et al. [31] present an extended version of the present study, including the full results from 61 qualitative interviews. Due to spatial limitations, we are unable to fully report the results of these interviews in the current paper, but we mention the most important results. In all instances, the mentioned interview results are based on [31]. The purpose of the qualitative interviews was to invite interviewees to present their views on and illustrate the themes and questions in the quantitative survey with concrete examples. A central purpose was to provide additional and contextual information about these issues. Ten private and 15 professional drivers from Norway were interviewed. Corresponding numbers from Greece were 16 and 20. Analyzing the interviews, we systematically compared each of the four groups to look for common patterns and individual differences on each of the four studied road safety behaviours, to obtain concrete and typical examples and contextual information that can shed light on important issues.

3. Results

3.1. Description of the Sample

The study sample includes 596 private car drivers and 216 professional drivers from Norway, and 286 private car drivers and 199 professional drivers from Greece. In Tables 1–4 the main characteristics of the survey sample are presented.

Table 1. Distribution of drivers per city/county and sector.

Group	County/Sector	Number	Share	Share of Males
Private Norway	Oslo	461	36%	59%
	Aust-Agder	91	7%	64%
	Finnmark	44	3%	50%
Private Greece	Athens	199	15%	64%
	Rhodes	87	7%	62%
Professional Norway	Bus	115	9%	93%
	HGV	101	8%	97%
Professional Greece	Bus	100	8%	100%
	HGV	99	8%	99%
Total	-	1297	100%	72%

Table 1 indicates, as expected, that the share of male drivers is between 90 and 100% in the groups of professional drivers from both countries. The share of males is slightly higher in the Greek sample in general: There are five percentage points more males in both the private and professional groups in the Greek sample. A Chi-square test involving the private drivers does not indicate significantly different gender distributions in the two countries: X2 (1, N = 882) = 2099, $p = 0.147$. A Chi-square test involving the professional drivers indicates significantly different distributions of gender in the two countries: X2 (1, N = 415) = 7772, $p = < 0.01$. The gender differences in the national samples are statistically significant at the 1% level.

Table 2 indicates a higher share of respondents in the oldest group in the Norwegian samples of professional and private drivers compared to the Greek samples. The tendency is the opposite for the second oldest group of drivers. A Chi-square test indicated that differences between the Greek and the Norwegian total groups are significant at the 1% level: X^2 (4, N = 1297) = 64,513, $p = < 0.01$. Comparing driver experience, there were higher shares in the group with the longest experience (>20 years) among the Norwegian drivers, but only for the private drivers.

Table 2. Distribution of drivers per group (professional/private) and age.

Nationality/Group	<26 Years	26–35	36–45	46–55	56+
Norwegian private	7%	27%	23%	18%	26%
Norwegian professional	1%	18%	22%	36%	23%
Greek Private	5%	23%	30%	28%	14%
Greek professional	0%	12%	36%	45%	8%
Norwegian total	5%	25%	23%	23%	25%
Greek total	3%	18%	32%	35%	12%
Total	5%	22%	26%	27%	20%

We obtained aggregated official data on private car license holders in Norway and Greece in order to evaluate the representativeness of our national samples. These data indicate a proportion of 51% males among Norwegian car license holders (59% in the survey), while the corresponding proportion for Greece was 66% (64% in the survey) (cf. Table 2). Thus, women are somewhat under-represented in the Norwegian private driver sample.

The aggregated data for age groups in the two countries (cf. Table 3) are not totally comparable to the age groups applied in Table 2, but they indicate that the proportions of car drivers of 55 years and older are under-represented in both the national samples, but especially in Greece. Drivers between 25 and 34 years are over-represented in both national samples. There were no data on the education level of the car license holders in the two countries.

Table 3. Aggregated data on private car license holders in Norway and Greece.

Age Groups	Norway	Greece
<25	8%	5%
25–34	16%	14%
35–44	18%	20%
45–54	20%	19%
55+	38%	42%
Gender: M	51%	66%

For the private drivers, questions were also included about their highest level of education. National categories were somewhat different, also including Lyceum (a type of high school; 14–18 years) in the Greek sample. To adapt the alternative to Greece, we categorized the answer alternatives into four: (1) Primary school (Norway 3%, Greece: 2%), (2) High school (Norway 22%, Greece: 44%), (3) 3–4 years university/college (Norway 36%, Greece: 28%), (4) >5 years university (Norway 40%, Greece: 25%). Thus, the level of education was higher in the Norwegian sample of private drivers.

Questions were also included about the type of car private drivers usually drive and how often they drive a car. Passenger car was the most prevalent type in the Greek sample (90%) compared to 50% in the Norwegian sample. The Norwegian sample also included considerable proportions of station wagon (29%) and sports utility vehicle (SUV) (15%). Additionally, respondents were asked whether they usually drive an electric car or a hybrid, and 18% in Oslo answered yes, while 5% in Aust-Agder and 0 in Finnmark did. Corresponding proportions for Greece were 5% on Rhodes and 3% in Athens.

Respondents were also asked how often they drive. Comparing the five geographical locations in the two countries, the results indicated that drivers in Oslo and in Norway in general drove less than the other groups. On Rhodes and Athens, 77% and 76% answered that they drive every day, respectively. Corresponding proportions for Norway were: 24% (Oslo), 43% (Aust-Agder), and 66% (Finnmark).

The bus drivers from Norway were recruited from four companies (including 25 drivers with an unknown company), while bus drivers in Greece were recruited from two companies. About half of the drivers in each national sample drove a local bus. The other halves in the national samples were unevenly distributed: the other half of the Greek respondents drove long distance, while the other half of the Norwegian drivers were distributed on long distance (16%), school bus (24%), and other types. Two surveys among professional HGV drivers from seven companies in Norway (and a group of drivers from unknown companies) and two companies in Greece were undertaken. Most of the HGV drivers were usually driving long distance (17% Norway (NO), 52% Greece (GR)), followed by a combination of long distance and distribution (35% NO, 24% GR) and distribution (12% NO, 24% GR). Table 4 presents numbers for kilometers, accidents, and accident risk for the four groups in the study.

Table 4. Estimated mean thousand kilometers (Kms) driven in the last two years with a car or heavy vehicles, including share and number of respondents who answered that they had experienced an accident in the last two years, total number of million kms, and estimated risk of accidents with property damage, based on self-reported numbers of kilometers and accidents.

Group	Kms	N	Std. Dev.	Accidents %	Accidents N	Mill Kms	ESTIMATED RISK
Private Norway	22	596	21.49	10%	57	13.1	4.4
Private Greece	22	286	11.42	16%	49	6.2	7.9
Professional Norway	97	216	79.85	17%	34	21.0	1.6
Professional Greece	122	196	73.24	36%	72	23.9	3.0

The proportion of 36% accident involvement in the professional Greek sample is surprisingly high. It is, however, important to note that, in this study, accidents refer to incidents that at least involve property damage. Thus, accidents may refer to events ranging from incidents involving broken wing mirrors to fatal accidents. In the Norwegian HGV sample, 37% usually drove dangerous goods, which is known to have a higher safety level than other HGV transport [2]. The accident risk of the Norwegian HGV drivers who drove dangerous goods in the sample was 0.5 accidents per million vehicle kilometers (three accidents per 6.3 million vehicle kms), compared to 0.9 for those who did not (seven accidents per 8.1 million vehicle kms).

It is difficult to compare the risk estimates in Table 4 with statistics based on more objective accident records, as they generally focus on other measures of exposure (billion population) and other types of incidents (fatal accidents). Nevertheless, the previously mentioned statistics of fatal accidents per billion population indicates that the risk in Greece is 3.5 times higher than in Norway. Our estimates of the risk of property damage accidents per million vehicle kilometers indicate that the risk is nearly 2 times higher among Greek drivers.

3.2. Road Safety Behaviours

3.2.1. Survey Results

The present section relates to the first aim of our study, which is to compare road safety behaviours among professional and private car drivers in Norway and Greece. More specifically, the section lays the foundation for testing Hypotheses 1–4. Previous research [22] has indicated that a two-factor solution was appropriate for the five DBQ items (aggressive violations and speeding) that we included in the study based on previous research [21]. We therefore conducted a confirmatory factor analysis (CFA) to examine the underlying factor structure of the five DBQ items measuring road safety behaviours (cf. Table 5). The tests indicated that the five items and the data were suitable for factor analysis.

Bartlett's test of sphericity (approx. Chi-square) was 1149.146 ($p < 0.001$). The Kaiser–Meyer–Olkin's measure of sampling adequacy showed a value of 0.647. The two first components had an Eigenvalue higher than 1, which explained a total of 66.4% of the variance. We used a principal component analysis (PCA) with Oblimin rotation, where we set the number of factors to 2 and the cutoff values of the factor loadings at 0.3. This produced the following result.

Table 5. Factor analysis results: road safety behaviours.

Item	Aggressive Violations	Over Speeding
(1) Sound your horn to indicate your annoyance to another road user	0.882	-
(2) Become angered by a certain type of driver and indicate your hostility by whatever means you can	0.845	-
(3) Pull out of a junction so far that the driver with right of way has to stop and let you out	0.632	-
(4) Disregard the speed limit on a residential road	-	0.839
(5) Disregard the speed limit on a motor way road	-	0.837

Based on the factor analysis in Table 5, we made an aggressive violations index based on the sum scores of the three items loading on this factor (Cronbach's Alpha: 0.698) (min 3, max 21), and an over speeding index based on the two items loading on this factor (Cronbach's Alpha: 0.591) (min 2, max 14).

Two additional and unrelated behaviour items were also included in our study "Drive when you suspect you might be over the legal blood alcohol limit" and "Drive without using a seat belt". These were not included in the factor analysis, as these items have not been found to be related to the two factors in Table 5 in previous studies, and as there are no substantial or theoretical reasons to assume that they are related to them. As noted, these two behaviours were included to test the hypothesis that they were more strongly correlated with the professional versus private dimension than nationality. Table 6 presents mean scores for the road safety behaviour variables.

Table 6. Mean scores for four road safety behaviour variables in the four groups: Aggressive violations (min: 3, max: 21), Over speeding (min: 2, max: 14), Driving under the influence (DUI) (min: 1, Max: 7) Driving without a seat belt (Min: 1, max: 7).

Group	Aggressive Violations	Over Speeding	Driving under the Influence	Driving without Using a Seat Belt
Private Norway	4.3	5.1	1.0	1.1
Professional Norway	4.7	4.5	1.1	1.5
Private Greece	5.7	5.1	1.4	2.4
Professional Greece	5.8	4.0	1.0	5.3
Total Norway	4.4	4.9	1.0	1.2
Total Greece	5.7	4.7	1.2	3.6
Correlation with accident involvement	0.102 ***	0.014	0.017	0.185 ***
Correlation with National RSC	0.376 ***	0.113 ***	0.252 ***	0.421 ***
Correlation with accident risk	0.098 ***	0.083 **	0.218 ***	−0.042

* $p < 0.1$, ** $p < 0.05$, *** $p < 0.01$.

We conducted post-hoc tests (Tukey) to examine whether the differences between the mean scores were significantly different, using one-way ANOVA (based on a variable with one value for each the four groups). In accordance with Hypothesis 1, we found a significantly higher score for aggressive violations in the Greek sample ($p = < 0.01$). Contrary to Hypothesis 2, we did not find significant differences between Norwegian and Greek drivers ($p = 0.210$) on the over speeding index.

Looking more specifically at the group scores on the aggressive violations index, we did not find significant differences between the private and professional drivers within each country, but we did for each group across countries (at the 1% level). This is in accordance with Hypothesis 3, and it could indicate different national RSCs within the countries, specified as patterns of behaviours shared by private and professional drivers.

Comparing means on driving under the influence variable, we only found significant differences between private drivers from Greece and all the other groups. This is partly in accordance with Hypothesis 4, as it indicates a higher prevalence of driving under the influence (DUI) among private drivers. Comparing means on the driving without a seatbelt variable, we found statistically significant differences between the scores of all the groups. This could also be interpreted to be in accordance with Hypothesis 4, as we found higher scores for professional drivers than for private drivers in both countries, although the difference between private and professional drivers is far higher in Greece than in Norway.

To examine possible interaction effects between the two variables (nationality and professional-private driver), we conducted two-way ANOVA analyses using the nationality and the professional versus private variables. The results show, as the mean scores indicate, interaction effects between nationality and professional-versus-private driver on driving under the influence of alcohol ($p = < 0.01$) and driving without seatbelt ($p = < 0.01$). This means that the effect of the professional versus private variable on these two behaviours is contingent on nationality. The p-value for the interaction tests involving aggressive violations was 0.278, while it was 0.246 for over speeding.

3.2.2. Results from the Qualitative Interviews

Aggressive Violations. The Greek private drivers described themselves and other Greek drivers as irritated in traffic. They explained this by pointing to challenging traffic conditions and time pressure. They mentioned that these conditions lead to tension and nervousness, while other road users' unpredictable driving gives them a constant sense of alertness and anxiety. They said that these are conditions that occur, if not every day, so very often. All the Greek bus drivers also mentioned that they often get angry with other drivers, but that they are trying to stay calm because they are professionals, and because they are also aware that they have passengers. Greek HGV drivers also mentioned that it is common in Greece to signal anger and irritation through inappropriate non-verbal gestures, inappropriate language, and honking. They also perceived that this has become worse due to the financial crisis; that Greek drivers have become more tense in the last few years of the financial crisis; and that it makes them more prone to "explode" in traffic. The majority of the Norwegian private car drivers mentioned that they sometimes get annoyed or angry when driving. However, it does not appear that this is a widespread characteristic of the driving of the Norwegian drivers we interviewed. First, they expected little irritation and anger from other drivers. Second, irritation and anger occurred relatively rarely among those we interviewed, and they did not refer to themselves as "irritated drivers", as Greek private car drivers did. The Norwegian drivers referred to aggressive drivers as exceptions requiring specific (psychological) explanations. Norwegian professional drivers also said that they could get irritated in traffic, especially as other drivers often show little understanding of, and patience with the behaviour and needs of heavy vehicles in traffic. They said, however, that they seldom show irritation in traffic; instead, they obtain an outlet for this when they talk to their colleagues, e.g., in their lunch breaks.

Over Speeding. All the Greek private drivers believed that over speeding often occurs, and that it is an important cause of accidents. The Greek bus drivers said that they drive below the speed limits, either because of the speed limiter and the tachograph, or because they have passengers on board, generally to avoid accidents. The Greek HGV drivers said that they drive slower than the speed limits in urban areas, and that they in some cases cross the speed limit on motorways. They also said that their choice of speed depends on time pressure and pressure from customers, or from management to deliver goods at a certain time. Norwegian private drivers asserted that drivers in Norway generally respect speed limits in residential areas, but that they often can drive slightly above the speed limit, for example on motorways. In addition, Norwegian HGV drivers mentioned that their managers influence their choice of speed, e.g., through fleet management systems and a focus on speed and driving style in their communication. Several also mentioned that their companies participate in programs focusing on traffic safety and driver behavior.

Driving under the Influence of Alcohol. The Greek private drivers referred to driving under the influence of alcohol as a common situation, both in Athens and on Rhodes, especially during the summer holidays with tourists. The majority of the interviewees said that they have seen, or know of, many cases of driving under the influence of alcohol. The Greek private drivers explained the relatively high incidence of DUI by saying that drivers often have the belief that they can drive equally safely even if they are influenced by alcohol, that the chances of being discovered by the police are small, that the distances are short, and that "there is little chance of an accident". In addition, they mentioned that, especially in Athens, taking a taxi home after drinking alcohol is a "foreign mentality". The Norwegian private drivers emphasized that driving under the influence of alcohol is very socially unacceptable, nor did they expect other drivers in Norway to drive after drinking alcohol. One mentioned that he would only do it if he was far away in the mountains, if someone was hurt, and their life depended on his choice. Such examples (e.g., "only if someone's life depended on it" versus "taking a taxi home after drinking alcohol is a foreign mentality") indicate the importance of descriptive norms, in the sense that they show differences in what is socially unacceptable in the Greek and Norwegian society. Our results indicate that it is even less accepted to drive under the influence of alcohol in Norway than in Greece. It seems that the descriptive norms concern "what one does, and what one does not", and the interviews indicate that this is strongly related to morality and identity, in that there are certain things one does not do because it is morally wrong. It seems that this is linked to feelings, morals, and identity, cf. "if someone's life depended on it". The Norwegian drivers emphasized that those who drive in an alcohol-influenced state are special cases of exemption, which often have to be "explained" by referring to "deviating personality traits". The qualitative data seem to indicate that the national dimension is very central to explaining differences in driving under the influence of alcohol. On the other hand, Norwegian interviewees also mentioned that they were aware of DUI from the media, from their own municipality, etc. They also said that this may be something that happens late in the night.

Driving without Using a Seat Belt. The Greek private drivers asserted that driving without a seat belt was relatively widespread in their society, because of: (a) drivers' excessive beliefs in their own skills and safety, (b) the chances of being discovered by the police are small, and (c) the distances are short, and therefore there is "little chance of an accident". They asserted that the same reasons explained why they believed that driving under the influence of alcohol was relatively widespread. The Greek private drivers stressed that the absence of an effective traffic police is the main cause of unsafe driving and traffic offenses. The Greek HGV drivers said that their managers did not necessarily require them to use seat belts. However, they believed that the use of seat belts in the Greek community has increased. Most interviewees reported relatively low seat belt use among HGV drivers, based on a perception that heavy vehicles act as protective shields in accidents. None of the Norwegian private drivers said that they were driving without using a seat belt. One of them said that this might have occurred in a few special cases: "Have been driving maybe 20 m down to the mailbox; it has happened. It is at the cottage in the countryside." The interviewees also believed that other private drivers in Norway generally use seat belts. Most of the interviewed Norwegian HGV drivers reported that their managers do not focus on their seat belt use, either because they take for granted that they use it, or because they see it as the driver's own responsibility. One of the interviewees said that he has

3.3. National Road Safety Culture

The present section relates to Hypothesis 5, assuming that we will see relatively similar scores comparing means for national RSC between the groups within countries, but significantly different when comparing groups across countries. The study includes nine items measuring national road safety culture, operationalized as descriptive norms. A previous study [22] indicated that a two-factor solution was appropriate for these nine items. We therefore conducted a confirmatory factor analysis (CFA) (cf. Table 7). The tests indicated that the five items and the data were suitable for factor analysis. Bartlett's test of sphericity (approx. Chi-square) was 6352.290 ($p < 0.001$). The Kaiser–Meyer–Olkin's measure of sampling adequacy showed a value of 0.870. The two first components had an Eigenvalue higher than 1, which explained a total of 68% of the variance. We used a principal component analysis (PCA) with Oblimin rotation, where we set the number of factors to 2 and the cutoff values of the factor loadings at 0.3.

Table 7. Factor analysis results: national road safety culture scales.

Item: ("When Driving in my Country, I Expect the Following Behaviour from Other Drivers:")	Aggression/Violations	Compliance/Politeness
(1) That they sound their horn to indicate their annoyance to another road user	0.854	-
(2) That they become angered by a certain type of driver and indicate their hostility by whatever means they can	0.852	-
(3) That they overtake a slow driver on the inside	0.824	-
(4) That they drive when they suspect they might be over the legal blood alcohol limit	0.792	-
(5) That they drive without using a seatbelt	0.771	-
(6) That they disregard the speed limit on a motor way road	0.725	-
(7) That they disregard the speed limit on a residential road	0.706	-
(8) That they respect and follow traffic rules	-	0.914
(9) That they are polite to other road users	-	0.882

We made a National RSC aggression/violations index based on the sum scores of the seven items loading on this factor in Table 8 (Cronbach's Alpha: 0.899) (min 7, max 49). We also made a National RSC compliance/politeness index based on the sum scores of the two items loading on this factor in Table 8 (Cronbach's Alpha: 0.783) (min 2, max 14). Table 9 shows results on the two national RSC indexes for the different groups.

Table 8. National Road safety culture indexes.

Nationality/Group	Aggression/Violations		Compliance/Politeness	
	Mean	Std.D	Mean	Std.D
Norwegian private	10.7	3.58	7.7	2.59
Norwegian professional	14.0	5.51	6.9	2.51
Greek Private	18.6	7.05	6.6	2.08
Greek professional	18.6	7.22	5.4	2.27
Norwegian total	11.6	4.42	7.5	2.59
Greek total	18.6	7.11	6.1	2.24
Total	14.2	6.53	7	2.55

Table 9. Linear regression analyses for three groups. Dependent variable: "Aggressive violations". Standardized beta coefficients.

Variables	Both Groups	Professional	Private
Gender (Male: 1, Female: 2)	−0.095 ***	−0.040	−0.092 ***
Age Group	−0.095 ***	−0.081 *	−0.093 ***
Nationality (Nor.: 1, Greek: 2)	0.022	0.08	−0.001
National RSC: Aggression/violations	0.288 ***	0.289 ***	0.122 ***
National RSC: Compliance/politeness	0.008	0.045	0.011
Rhodes (Other = 1, Rhodes = 2)	0.123 ***	-	0.089 **
Organizational safety culture	-	−0.119 **	-
Education	-	-	−0.061 *
Professional Greek (Other: 1, Prof. Greek: 2)	0.053	-	-
Time pressure/stress	-	0.125 **	-
Dangerous goods (Other: 1, Dang. goods: 2)	-	−0.027	-
Station wagon (1: Other, 2: Station wagon)	-	-	−0.005
Peers' RSC	-	-	0.287 ***
Sector focus on safety	-	0.104 *	-
Adjusted R^2	0.168	0.146	0.223

* $p < 0.1$, ** $p < 0.05$, *** $p < 0.01$.

We conducted post-hoc tests (Tukey) to examine whether the differences between the mean scores were significantly different using one-way ANOVA. We did not find significant differences between the private and professional drivers within Greece on the Aggression/violations index, but we found significant differences between private and professional drivers in Norway (at the 1% level). The similar scores for Greek professional and private drivers on the Aggression/violations index is in accordance with Hypothesis 5, but the significantly different scores for the Norwegian drivers are not. Comparing scores on the Compliance/politeness index, we found statistically significant differences between all groups except private drivers in Greece and professional drivers in Norway. This is not in accordance with Hypothesis 5. We return to this below.

3.4. Factors Influencing Road Safety Behaviours

In this section, we conduct 12 regression analyses when testing Hypotheses 6–8, in accordance with the second aim of our study. We conduct three analyses for each road safety behaviour variable: one for both professional and private drivers in Norway and Greece, one for only professional drivers in both countries, and one for only private car drivers in both countries. First, we examine factors influencing aggressive violations, then over speeding, driving under the influence, and finally a lack of seat belt use.

3.4.1. Aggressive Violations

In Table 9, we show results from three linear regression analyses, where we examine the variables predicting aggressive violations in three groups, testing Hypotheses 6–8: (1) both professional and private drivers in Norway and Greece, (2) only professional drivers in both countries, and (3) only private drivers in both countries. The first five independent variables in the three models are the same, then variables that are unique to either professional drivers or private drivers are introduced. The table presents the standardized beta coefficients. The contributions of the different independent variables on the dependent variables can therefore be compared directly. The scores on the dependent variable vary between 3 and 21.

If we look at the first five variables that are similar in the three models, we first see that the national road safety culture (RSC) measured as aggression/violations has the strongest contribution in the first two analyses (both groups and professionals) and has the second strongest contribution in the third model (private). This indicates that respondents who expect more aggressive and risky driving from drivers from their own country drive more aggressively themselves. We have seen that this applies to the Greek respondents.

Second, we see that age contributes significantly in all analyses, and indicates less aggressive driving with increased age. Third, gender contributes significantly in two of the analyses, indicating that women are drive less aggressively. A fourth important finding is that nationality does not contribute significantly. It may therefore appear that the national influence on driving behaviour in this case is primarily mediated through national RSC.

Focusing on the professional drivers, we see that high (positive) organizational safety culture scores are related to less aggressive violations and vice versa. This indicates that (the effect of nationality on) aggressive road safety behavior can be prevented to some extent by working systematically with organizational safety culture in transport companies. As expected, time pressure/stress contributes to an increased occurrence of aggressive violations among the professional drivers. Sector focus on safety also contributes significantly to increased prevalence of aggressive violations, and this is difficult to explain. This may due to the fact that the Greek professional drivers report a higher focus on safety and a higher degree of aggressive driving. We found that national RSC generally was more important for the professional drivers' possible aggressive violations than work-related and organizational variables, although it is important to point out that organizational safety culture also contributed significantly.

Focusing on the private car drivers, we first and foremost see that peers' road safety culture is the variable with the strongest contribution. This variable was also included in the analyses for both groups. The scale measuring peer RSC was based on the same items as the national RSC scale, addressing expectations to "your friends who regularly drive a car". Respondents answering the latter were filtered based on the question: "Do you have friends who regularly drive a car?" (only a total of 30 respondents answered no). Private car drivers from Rhodes score significantly higher on the aggressive violations index (7.1 points versus 4.8 points for the other groups and 5.1 points for Athens). Education contributes negatively to aggressive driving, indicating less aggressive violations with increasing education. Station wagon does not contribute significantly. The rationale for this variable was that results indicated the lowest level of aggressive violations for station wagon (4.3 points) compared to all other private car types (4.9 points).

Comparing the adjusted R^2 values, we see that the analysis with both groups explains about 17% of the variation in the aggressive violations of the private car and professional drivers, and about 15% in the variation of the professional drivers' aggressive violations. The analysis involving only the private car drivers has somewhat higher explanatory power and explains 22% of the variation in their aggressive violations.

3.4.2. Over Speeding

In Table 10, we show results from three hierarchical, linear regression analyses, where we examine the variables predicting over speeding in three groups.

Table 10. Linear regression analyses for three groups. Dependent variable: "Over speeding". Standardized beta coefficients.

Variables	Both Groups	Professional	Private
Gender (Male: 1, Female: 2)	−0.043	0.052	−0.085 **
Age Group	0.070 **	0.081	0.093 ***
Nationality (Nor.: 1, Greek: 2)	−0.137 ***	−0.120 *	−0.236 ***
National RSC: Aggression/violations	0.140 ***	0.117 **	0.129 ***
National RSC: Compliance/politeness	0.031	0.007	0.036
Rhodes (Other = 1, Rhodes = 2)	0.181 ***	-	0.139 ***
Organizational safety culture	-	0.100 *	-
Education	-	-	−0.051
Professional Greek (Other: 1, Prof. Greek: 2)	−0.052	-	-
Time pressure/stress	-	0.041	-
Dangerous goods (Other: 1, Dang. goods: 2)	-	−0.012	-
Station wagon (1: Other, 2: Station wagon)	-	-	−0.008
Peers' RSC	-	-	0.167 ***
Sector focus on safety	-	−0.006	-
Adjusted R^2	0.058	0.012	0.089

* $p < 0.1$ ** $p < 0.05$, *** $p < 0.01$.

Looking at the first five variables that are similar in the three models, we first see that nationality seems to be the independent variable with the strongest contribution in the analyses. This variable contributes negatively, which means that Greek nationality was related to less over speeding. Second, we see that national road safety culture (aggression/violations) contributes significantly in all analyses. This indicates a relationship between the respondents' speed behaviour and the violations and aggression that they attribute to other drivers in their own country. Third, we see that age contributes significantly in two of the analyses, indicating more over speeding with increased age. This is difficult to explain, and may be due to more over speeding at a somewhat higher age in the Norwegian sample. Fourth, gender contributes significantly and negatively in the analysis of the private drivers, indicating that women are less likely to over speed controlled for nationality, age, education, etc.

Examining the variables that influence the professional drivers' over speeding, we see that organizational safety culture contributes positively. This is difficult to explain, and may be related to national differences in over speeding and organizational safety culture (i.e., high levels of both in the Norwegian sample). None of the other work-related or organizational variables contribute significantly.

Nationality is the variable contributing most strongly (and negatively) to private drivers' over speeding. This reflects lower levels of over speeding among the Greek respondents. Peers' road safety culture has the second strongest contribution, indicating a relationship between respondents' behaviour and their perceptions of the behavior of their own friends who drive cars regularly. The variable with the third strongest contribution to over speeding is Rhodes. This suggests more over speeding among respondents on Rhodes, controlled for the other variables in the model, including gender and age. This variable was included because Rhodes respondents had the highest average score on the over speeding index (7 points compared to the 4.8-point average). Since we control for gender and age, the higher score on Rhodes does not necessarily appear to be due to sample effects. It is interesting that the influence of Rhodes on over speeding is the opposite of the influence of nationality (i.e., less over speeding for Greek drivers, but more over speeding for Greek island drivers). This indicates that drivers from Rhodes are different from the other Greek drivers in the sample.

Comparing the adjusted R^2 values, we see that the analysis with both groups explains about 6% of the variation in the over speeding of the private car and professional drivers. This is low and indicates that the model did not provide a good prediction of the factors influencing respondents' over speeding. The value is even lower in the analysis that only involved the professional drivers: 0.012, which means that this analysis explained 1% of the variation. This is very low. The analysis that only involves the private car drivers explains 9% of the variation in their over speeding.

3.4.3. Driving under the Influence of Alcohol

In Table 11, we show results from three hierarchical, linear regression analyses, where we examine the variables predicting driving under the influence of alcohol in three groups.

Table 11. Linear regression analyses for three groups. Dependent variable: "Driving when you suspect that your blood alcohol content may be higher than the legal limit". Standardized beta coefficients.

Variables	Both Groups	Professional	Private
Gender (Male: 1, Female: 2)	−0.086 ***	−0.062	−0.077 **
Age Group	−0.041	−0.096 **	−0.009
Nationality (Nor.: 1, Greek: 2)	0.144 ***	−0.240 ***	0.119 ***
National RSC: Aggression/violations	0.186 ***	0.282 ***	0.055
National RSC: Compliance/politeness	0.017	0.068	0.005
Rhodes (Other = 1, Rhodes = 2)	0.117 ***	-	0.097 **
Organizational safety culture	-	0.068	-
Education	-	-	−0.004
Professional Greek (Other: 1, Prof. greek: 2)	−0.210 ***	-	-
Time pressure/stress	-	0.064	-
Dangerous goods (Other: 1, Dang. goods: 2)	-	−0.088 *	-
Station wagon (1: Other, 2: Station wagon)	-	-	0.009
Peers' RSC	-	-	0.192 ***
Sector focus on safety	-	0.060	-
Adjusted R²	0.119	0.085	0.142

* $p < 0.1$, ** $p < 0.05$, *** $p < 0.01$.

Looking at the first five variables that are similar in the three analyses, we first see that nationality contributes strongly in all the analyses. Interestingly, the influence of nationality is different for private and professional drivers: it is positive for the private drivers and negative for the professional drivers. This indicates that, when we look only at the professional drivers, being Greek is related to a lower prevalence of driving under the influence (AVG: NO=1.1, GR=1.0), while it is opposite for the private drivers (AVG: NO=1.0, GR=1.4). We also saw this in the analysis of both groups, where Greek nationality contributed positively, while the professional Greek variable contributed negatively.

Second, we see that national road safety culture (aggression/violations) contributes significantly in the first two analyses, but not in the analysis that only includes private drivers. The effect of national road safety culture indicates that respondents who report to sometimes drive under the influence of alcohol expect a higher degree of aggression and violation among drivers in their own country and vice versa.

Third, gender contributes significantly and negatively to the analysis of both groups and in the analysis of the private drivers. This indicates that women drive less under the influence of alcohol, controlled for nationality, age, education, etc. The result that the effect of gender is not significant for the professional drivers is probably due to low gender variation in this group: the professional drivers mostly consist of men.

Focusing on the professional drivers, it can first be mentioned that the analyses indicate that being a professional (Greek) driver is the variable that is most strongly related to the lower incidences of driving under the influence of alcohol. Driving dangerous goods contributes significantly and negatively, which indicates a lower degree of driving under the influence among drivers of dangerous goods. Age contributes significantly and negatively, indicating a lower degree of driving under the influence with increased age. We found, however, that national road safety culture and nationality generally were more important for the professional drivers' potential driving under the influence of alcohol than work-related and organizational variables. Based on the analyses, it is therefore difficult to point to the factors that might explain the strong influence of being a professional driver on (low incidence of) driving under the influence of alcohol. We may assume that it is probably related to professionalism (there are probably fewer people who drink at work than in their leisure time; especially people who drive at work, as this involves a higher accident risk) and the work context (driving under the influence is probably related to parties, often on weekends, evenings, and nights).

Focusing on the private drivers, we see that national RSC does not contribute significantly. Peers' road safety culture was the variable with the strongest contribution to the private drivers' potential driving under the influence of alcohol, in addition to (Greek) nationality and the variable Greek island. The significant contribution of peers' road safety culture indicates a relationship between the potential driving under the influence of alcohol of private drivers and the level of violations that they attributed to their own friends who regularly drive a car. Additionally, we see that being a Greek private car driver is related to a higher degree of driving under the influence, and being a car driver on Rhodes in the sample is related to an even higher incidence of driving under the influence. Being a woman is related to a lower degree of driving under the influence of alcohol.

When we compare the adjusted R^2 values, we see that the analysis with both groups explains about 12% of the variation in the private and professional drivers driving under the influence of alcohol. This is relatively low. The value is somewhat lower in the analysis that only involves the professional drivers: 0.085, which means that this analysis explains 9% of the variation in their driving under the influence. The analysis only involving the private drivers explains 14% of the variation in their driving under the influence.

3.4.4. Driving without Using a Seat Belt

In Table 12, we show results from three hierarchical, linear regression analyses, where we examine the variables predicting driving without a seat belt in the three groups.

Table 12. Linear regression analyses for three groups. Dependent variable: "Drive without a seat belt". Standardized beta coefficients.

Variables	Both Groups	Professional	Private
Gender (Male: 1. Female: 2)	−0.070 ***	−0.025	−0.091 ***
Age Group	0.000	−0.015	0.012
Nationality (Nor.: 1, Greek: 2)	0.159 ***	0.685 ***	0.214 ***
National RSC: Aggression/violations	0.177 ***	0.132 ***	0.184***
National RSC: Compliance/politeness	−0.006	−0.004	0.008
Rhodes (Other = 1, Rhodes = 2)	-	-	0.064 *
Organizational safety culture	-	−0.145 ***	-
Education	-	-	−0.136 ***
Professional Greek (Other: 1. Prof. greek: 2)	0.489 ***	-	-
Time pressure/stress	-	−0.078 **	-
Dangerous goods (Other: 1. Dang. goods: 2)	-	−0.034	-
Station wagon (1: Other. 2: Station wagon)	-	-	0.009
Peers' RSC	-	-	0.148 ***
Sector focus on safety	-	0.028	-
Oslo (Other = 1. Oslo = 2)	−0.040	-	-
Adjusted R^2	0.515	0.518	0.293

* $p < 0.1$, ** $p < 0.05$, *** $p < 0.01$.

When we look at the first five variables that are similar in the three models, we see, first of all, that nationality contributes strongly in all the analyses, especially in the analyses that include only the professional drivers. The effect of nationality means that being a Greek driver is related to a higher incidence of driving without a seat belt. This especially applies to the professional Greek drivers. Second, we see that national road safety culture (aggression/violations) contributes significantly in all analyses, indicating that respondents who expect a higher degree of aggression and violations among drivers in their own country report a higher degree of driving without a seat belt, and vice versa. Third, gender significantly and negatively contributes to the analysis of both groups and the private drivers. This indicates that women are more likely to wear belts, controlled for nationality, age, education, etc. The fact that the effect of gender is not significant in the analyses only including the professional drivers is probably due to the fact that the professional drivers are mostly men.

Focusing on the professional drivers, the analyses indicate that being a professional (Greek) driver is the variable that is most strongly related to driving without a safety belt. This was also evident in our comparisons of the group means on this variable. We created this variable for the analyses of "Both groups", as we saw that the professional Greek drivers had the highest incidence of driving without a seat belt. Organizational safety culture negatively contributes to driving without a safety belt. This indicates that a positive organizational safety culture is related to lower prevalence of driving without a safety belt and vice versa. This indicates that (the effect of nationality on) unsafe road behavior to some extent can be prevented by working systematically with organizational safety culture in transport companies. Drivers' experience of time pressure and stress in their work also contributes (negatively) to less driving without a safety belt. This is hard to explain. We found, however, that nationality and national road safety culture were more important for the professional drivers' potential driving without a safety belt than work-related and organizational variables.

Nationality and national road safety culture are also the most important explanatory variables in the analyses of the private drivers' potential to drive without a seat belt. However, these analyses also indicate that peers' road safety culture contributes significantly to private drivers' potential lacking seat belt use, in addition to education and Rhodes. The importance of peers' road safety culture indicates a relationship between private car drivers' potential lacking seat belt use, and the extent of road safety violations that they attribute to their friends. In addition, the results indicate that the prevalence of driving without a seat belt is lower with increased education, controlled for the other variables in the analysis. Being a private car driver on Rhodes in the sample is also related to driving without a safety belt, but the variable is only significant at the 10% level and contributes weakly. Finally, we see that being a woman is related to a lower degree of driving without a seat belt, controlled for the other variables in the analyses of the private drivers.

Comparing the adjusted R_2 values, we see that the analysis with both groups explains about 52% of the variation in the private and professional drivers' lack of seat belt use. This is relatively high. The value was about the same for the analysis that only involved the professional drivers, while it was 0.293, or 29%, for the private car drivers. This difference is probably due to the strong relationship between nationality and the private versus professional dimension that we see from the standardized beta coefficients in the first two analyses in Table 11.

3.5. Factors Influencing Accident Involvement

In this section, we conduct three logistic regression analyses when testing Hypotheses 9–12, in accordance with the third aim of the study. A total of 214 respondents had been involved in an accident in the course of the last two years. This applies to 10% of the private Norwegian drivers, 17% of the private Greek drivers, 16% of the professional Norwegian drivers, and 36% of the Greek professional drivers. Table 13 shows logistic regression analyses of the variables influencing accident involvement. Choosing behavioural variables potentially predicting respondents' accident involvement to include in the model, we only included aggressive violations. The first reason for this is that we only wanted to include variables related to the occurrence of accidents, and not the severity. This excludes failure to use a seat belt. Second, we chose the most important variable related to the occurrence of accidents. Aggressive violations was the only variable that was significantly (although weakly) correlated with accidents in our study (cf. Table 5).

Table 13. Logistic regression analyses for three groups. Dependent variable: "Accidents (No = 0, Yes = 1)". Beta values.

Variables	Both Groups	Professional	Private
Gender (Female = 0, Male = 1)	0.098	0.355	−0.042
Age group	−0.056	−0.067	−0.094
1000 km driven	0.000	−0.001	0.002
Aggressive violations	0.048 *	0.036	0.032
Nationality (Greek = 0, Norw. = 1)	−0.422 **	−1.052 ***	−0.585 **
Subgroup (professional Greek = 0, Other = 1)	−0.980 **	-	-
Time pressure/stress	-	0.217 **	-
Rhodes (Other = 1, Rhodes = 2)	-	-	−0.115
Dangerous goods (Other: 2, Dang. goods: 2)	-	0.611	-
Sector focus on safety	-	−0.070	-
Nagelkerke R	0.083	0.122	0.027

* $p < 0.1$, ** $p < 0.05$, *** $p < 0.01$.

Although the presented beta values cannot be compared directly, as their size is contingent on the coding of the variables, the contributions of the three significant variables in Step 6 can be compared, as the two most important are dichotomous, and as the third only contributed significantly at the 10% level. The subgroup "professional Greek" respondents (bus, HGV) was the variable with the strongest contribution in the model including both groups, probably as these had the highest proportion of accidents (36%) compared to the other groups. There are reasons to hypothesize that this could be due to their mileage, but, surprisingly, this variable does not contribute significantly in the model. (It contributes, however, significantly if the variable professional Greek driver is excluded.)

Nationality contributed significantly and negatively, reflecting the lower proportion of accidents among Norwegian respondents. We also saw a lower incidence of aggressive violations among Norwegian drivers. However, the relationship between nationality and accidents is also due to other national conditions, as nationality also contributes significantly when controlling for aggressive violations. The third most important variable in the model is the index for aggressive violations, but it contributes less than the other two variables. The fact that this variable has a lower B value than the other two statistically significant independent variables may be because aggressive violations has more values (min: 3, max: 21) than the other two significant variables, which have only two values. The Nagelkerke R-value is 0.083. Thus, the model explains 8% of the variation in respondents' accident involvement.

Focusing on the professional drivers, we see that nationality contributes negatively and significantly, and that time pressure/stress contributes significantly and positively. This means that the analysis shows that increases in experienced time pressure and stress for bus and goods drivers is related to a higher prevalence of accident involvement. It is surprising that the variable dangerous goods does not contribute significantly. Nor does sector focus on safety. In the analyses involving only private drivers, only nationality contributes significantly. The variable Greek island was included because this group had the highest incidence of accident involvement among private drivers, but this variable does not contribute significantly in the analyses.

4. Discussion

The aims of the present study were to: (1) Compare the road safety behaviours among professional and private drivers in Norway and Greece; (2) Examine factors influencing road safety behaviours, focusing especially on national road safety culture; and (3) Examine the influence of road safety behaviours and other factors (e.g., demographic and work-related variables) on accident involvement.

4.1. Road Safety Culture Measured as Shared Patterns of Behaviour

First, we hypothesized that there would be more aggressive violations in the Greek sample than in the Norwegian sample (Hypothesis 1), as indicated by the research of Özkan et al. [20] and Warner et al. [21]. Our results supported this hypothesis. Our second hypothesis was that there would be more over speeding in the Norwegian sample than the Greek sample (Hypothesis 2), also in line with previous results from Özkan et al. [20] and Warner et al. [21]. The results did not support this hypothesis. Third, we hypothesized that some safety behaviours (i.e., aggressive violations and over speeding) would be more similar among private and professional drivers within the national samples, than among professional and private drivers across the national samples (Hypothesis 3), indicating different national RSC in the two countries (shared patterns of behaviour between private and professional drivers within countries). Our results supported this hypothesis when it comes to aggressive violations, but not when it comes to over speeding.

4.2. Road Safety Culture Measured as Descriptive Norms

Greek professional and private drivers had similar mean scores on the national RSC Aggression/ violations index, in accordance with Hypothesis 5, but Norwegian professional and private drivers had significantly different mean scores on this index. The latter does not support our hypothesis. In accordance with Hypothesis 5, we also expected relationships between respondents' behaviours and national RSC, especially on the variables that we primarily hypothesized to vary according to nationality. The results from the regression analyses supported this Hypothesis: national RSC Aggression/violations was one of the most important variables in the analyses including both private and professional drivers.

Comparing scores on the RSC Compliance/politeness index, we found statistically significant differences between all groups except private drivers in Greece and professional drivers in Norway. This was not in accordance with Hypothesis 5. On the contrary, this seemed to indicate the importance of similar experiences and viewpoints among professional drivers across countries and private drivers across countries. In both countries, private drivers scored higher on this index, indicating that they attributed more Compliance/politeness to other drivers in their country than professional drivers did. This could be due to the fact that professional drivers have different experiences, positions, and roles from private drivers. Results from the qualitative interviews support this interpretation: professional drivers in both countries complained about other drivers' lacking understanding of and patience with heavy vehicles in traffic. Professional drivers drive larger and slower vehicles, which often require more cooperation from other drivers, e.g., when entering the road (this especially applies to buses).

4.3. Road Safety Behaviours Varying According to the Professional Versus Private Dimension

Our fourth hypothesis was that some behaviours, i.e., driving under the influence and seat belt use [38,39], would be more similar between private drivers and professional drivers across countries, indicating that being a private or professional driver would be more important than nationality in these instances. Comparing means for driving under the influence variable, we only found significant differences between private drivers from Greece and all the other groups. This was in line with what we hypothesized, but it only applied to Greece. Comparing means on the driving without seatbelt variable, we found less seatbelt use for professional drivers in both countries, although the difference between private and professional drivers was greater in Greece than in Norway. This could be due to several different factors. It is known that the difference between private and professional drivers' seat belt wearing used to be greater in Norway than suggested by Table 7, and the little difference currently is generally attributed to successful safety efforts among companies, trade organizations, and authorities. In 2009, a bit over half of the heavy vehicle drivers in Norway wore a seatbelt, while the proportion was nearly 90% in 2015 [39]. Our results indicated statistically significant interaction effects for both seat belt use and driving under the influence. This means that the effect of the professional versus private variable on these two behaviours is contingent on nationality. The differences between groups within countries on these variables follow national patterns. This is also indicated in the regression analyses.

4.4. Factors Influencing Road Safety Behaviours

The reason that we hypothesized that some types of road safety behaviours would vary according to the professional versus private dimension was that we assumed that these behaviours primarily would be influenced by variables located at these analytical levels rather than at the national level. Our sixth hypothesis was that the safety behaviours of professional drivers would be influenced by work-related variables, such as organizational safety culture [12,14], experienced time pressure and stress [12,13] and (sub)sector, or focus on safety [2,57] (Hypothesis 6). The analyses for the professional drivers indicated that national RSC generally was more important than organizational and work-related factors in predicting their road safety behaviours. We found, however, that organizational safety culture also was an important variable influencing the safety behaviour of the professional drivers, indicating that a positive organizational safety culture may reduce unsafe behaviours, and perhaps also the (negative) effect of national RSC on road safety behaviours. Work pressure contributed to increased aggressive violations, and was significantly higher (1 point on a 5-point scale) for the Greek HGV drivers. Gender was not an important variable in the analyses of professional drivers due to low variation in the sample, and increasing age was related to less aggressive violations and less driving under the influence (cf. Hypothesis 8).

Seventh, we hypothesized that the safety behaviours of private drivers would be influenced by factors such as the road safety culture in their community [19] or in their peer groups [50] and level of education [35] (Hypothesis 7). The separate analyses for the private car drivers generally indicated, in accordance with Nævestad et al. [50], that peer RSC was the strongest predictor of all safety behaviours, except lacking seat belt use, followed by nationality and national RSC. In accordance with Sucha et al. [35], education contributed negatively to aggressive violations and lacking seat belt use, indicating less of these behaviours with increasing levels of education. Gender also contributed negatively, indicating generally less violations among female drivers (cf. [34]) (cf. Hypothesis 8). Rhodes contributed significantly in all the analyses of private drivers' behaviours, with higher levels of unsafe behaviours. Previous research has suggested the importance of geographical areas or communities as a source of road safety culture [4,19,49].

4.5. The Influence of Safety Behaviours and Other Factors on Accident Involvement

Ninth, we hypothesized that drivers' accident involvement would be influenced by their safety behaviours (e.g., aggressive violations) (Hypothesis 9). In accordance with our hypothesis and previous research [21], we found that aggressive violations influenced drivers' self-reported accident involvement, but it was only significant at the 10% level.

Tenth, in line with previous research, we hypothesized that drivers' accident involvement would be influenced by demographic variables, such as age, gender, and nationality (Hypothesis 10). Our results indicated, however, that neither age nor gender contributed significantly, contrary to previous research [41,42]. The results, however, supported Hypothesis 10, when it comes to nationality, as we found a relationship between nationality and accident involvement, indicating a higher accident involvement among Greek drivers. Previous studies also find nationality [36] or country [26,40] to predict drivers' accident risk. As discussed, this relationship is to some extent due to aggressive violations, but only partly, as the contribution of nationality still is considerable although we control for aggressive violations. Thus, this relationship also seems to be due to other national variables that we have been unable to measure. This indicates an important area for future research.

The non-significant relationship between drivers' accident involvement and mileage is in contrast to Hypothesis 11 and previous research (e.g., [2]). It was especially important to control for this in our study, as the annual average mileage of private and professional drivers is substantially different. (Mileage, however, contributed significantly in the model for both groups until the variable professional drivers was included.) It should also be noted that mileage is closely related to experience, which also is closely related to safety behaviours and accident risk [56,58,59] The professional drivers with a higher mileage level thereby have far higher levels of experience than the private drivers. We have unfortunately not been able to measure the effect of mileage controlled for experience in the present paper, and this indicates an issue for future research.

Twelfth, we hypothesized that work-related variables, such as time pressure and stress, sector, and framework conditions, would influence the accident risk of professional drivers (Hypothesis 12). In accordance with previous research, the results indicate a significant relationship between professional drivers' accident involvement and perceived time pressure and stress [1]. The professional Greek drivers, especially the goods drivers, mentioned in the qualitative interviews that their behaviours may be influenced by stress and time pressure. More research is needed.

4.6. Which Factors Contribute to the Existence of National Road Safety Cultures?

Interviewees underlined that norms prescribing road safety behaviours are created in road user interaction. This is in line with previous research, which indicates that shared norms continually are created and recreated through interaction among road users in traffic [19,20,60]. Discussing how different national RSC may come about, interviewees also mentioned several factors influencing the interaction. Road infrastructure is a potential factor influencing national RSC that was mentioned in the qualitative interviews. Interviewees related the poor(er) Greek road infrastructure to the financial crisis in Greece. This is in line with previous research [20], indicating that road infrastructure may set the premise for road user interaction. It is conceivable that poorly marked roads, poorly designed junctions, roads with a capacity that is too low, etc. may affect the quality of road user interaction negatively and create frustration and aggression. This is an issue for future research. Another important factor potentially influencing national RSC that was underlined by the interviewees and also previous research is the level of enforcement [20]. There is a close relationship between the level of enforcement in countries and road user behaviours [2]. Thus, if drivers in a country (or a region) perceive that some types of violations not are enforced in practice by the police, it is likely that these types of violations may be more prevalent. Our results indicate less respect for traffic rules in the Greek samples, which could be related to the level of police enforcement. Results from the qualitative interviews strongly support this, and the Greek interviewees underlined the importance of insufficient enforcement for unsafe driver behaviours in their country. Future research should examine how such different enforcement practices may give rise to different national (or regional) RSCs. Additionally, it is not unreasonable to expect that national RSC, defined partly as our expectations of other road users, to some extent can be "normalized" in formal driver training. This was also mentioned by some of the private drivers in the qualitative interviews, and it indicates an area for future research.

Another factor that should be taken into account when discussing how national RSC may come about in interaction is the composition of road users who interact in the road systems. Our study indicates that demographic characteristics (e.g., gender, age, level of education) influence drivers' behaviours. Thus, an ageing driver population (e.g., like in Norway) is likely to influence drivers' behaviour, interaction, and thus RSC. Moreover, the composition of types of road users (e.g., vulnerable road users, motor cycles, heavy vehicles) is likely to influence interaction. In this respect, it should be mentioned that the Greek road context generally includes more powered two wheelers compared to the Norwegian road context. This could influence interaction and thus perhaps also national RSC. Finally, a factor mentioned by both private and professional Greek drivers in the qualitative interviews was the influence of the financial crisis on the Greek driving culture [31]. Both professional and private Greek interviewees asserted that, because of the financial crisis, Greek drivers were more tense and uptight. Several mentioned that, especially during the last years of the financial crisis, nerves were uptight, so all drivers explode much more easily while driving.

4.7. The Relationship between National RSC and National Accident Records

Our study indicates that national RSC is important, as it is related to road safety behaviours, which in turn is related to accident involvement. Above, we discussed the factors influencing national RSC. Figure 1 provides an illustration of possible relationships that should be examined in future research, based on the data in the present project.

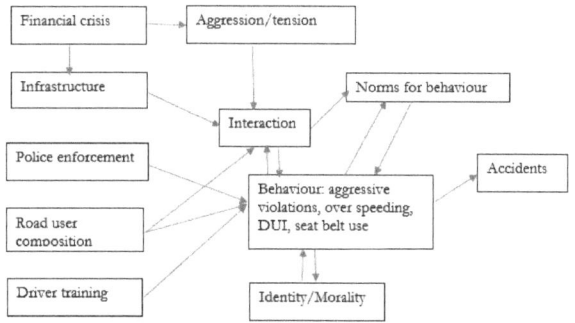

Figure 1. Illustration of possible relationships that should be examined in future research, based on the data in the present study.

The key question in the discussion of the relationship between national RSC and national road safety records is whether, or to what extent, national RSC is a cause of unsafe behaviours inducing a higher accident risk, or a symptom of a number of factors that contribute to negative RSC, negative behavior, and accidents. As indicated by Figure 1, our results do not indicate that road safety culture can provide the whole explanation of the different safety records in Norway and Greece, but that it appears to be part of and reflect on a larger picture of composite and complex factors. Above, we discussed six factors that contribute to creating a national RSC. Many of these factors are already used as key explanations for why we find variation between national accident statistics. The unique contribution of the present study is that we also associate these factors with shared patterns of behavior in traffic and shared norms of what is "normal" and expected of road users in different countries (i.e., national RSC). However, when discussing the importance of national RSC, it is important to remember that many other national factors also influence driving behaviour and its consequences (e.g., road safety campaigns, education, road design, traffic density, weather, fuel costs, vehicle fleet, enforcement (e.g., photo radar), and penalties for violations, etc.). These are factors that we have been unable to focus on in the present study. As noted, the logistic regression analysis indicated that the contribution of nationality to accident involvement still was considerable even though we controlled for aggressive violations.

4.8. Policy Implications

The relationships depicted in Figure 1 also provide an opportunity to discuss implications for policy, or how the knowledge about national RSC can be employed in efforts to improve road safety. As far as we see it, at least three general approaches can be applied as a point of departure. First, given the importance of interaction for national RSC, including the five factors influencing interaction, one way of improving national RSC (in an attempt to also improve behaviour and accidents) could be to target the five factors influencing the interaction among road users. Relevant questions in this respect are, e.g., Which factors are possible to influence? (How) do the factors interact? What are the expected outcomes? Which is the most important factor?

A second relevant approach that can be employed is to attempt to change the norms directly, e.g., through campaigns. Relevant questions in this respect are, e.g., How do social norms for road safety behaviour come about? To what extent is it possible to change such norms through other ways than the interaction processes in which (we assume) that they are created? How should it be done? To what extent are such norms an independent "social force"? The latter question concerns the extent to which norms for behaviour remain unchanged (in our minds) although the factors that contributed to them in the first place change, or whether behaviour and norms "follow" from infrastructure, police enforcement, and education. Although infrastructure and training can influence the interaction, it is also conceivable that the interaction itself creates a dynamic where new norms are developed (cf. [60]), which are more or less safe and which do not necessarily "follow" the infrastructure. For example, we saw that the respondents and those interviewed on Rhodes report other behavioral patterns and norms of behavior than the other respondents. Likewise, certain social groups may develop certain norms prescribing unsafe road behaviors, despite good training, infrastructure, and police enforcement. Our analyses show, for example, the importance of peers' road safety culture for their own behavior.

A third relevant approach is to target the relationship between norms for behaviour and behaviours through information campaigns, focusing on the descriptive norms mechanism. The underlying idea behind the social norms approach to interventions [3,53] is to remove false consensus effects supporting risky behaviour by informing risk groups about the actual prevalence of risky behaviour of their peers. This approach has successfully been employed in traffic safety interventions (e.g., [61]). As noted by Nævestad et al. [50], this approach may, however, not work if road users at risk have fairly correct perceptions of their peers' (un)safe behaviour. This could be the case in high-risk subcultures, which may be based on and defined by risky behaviours.

4.9. Methodological Limitations and Issues for Future Research

4.9.1. Conceptualization and Specification of the Main Variables

A limitation of the study is that the main variables were measured by means of a relatively small number of questions. It can also be argued that the underlying nature of some of these is narrow in scope [22]. This applies, for instance, to the road safety behaviour scale and our conceptualization of national RSC. We specified national RSC as shared patterns of behaviour and descriptive norms, based on a few key DBQ items that had been found important in previous research. The DBQ was, however, not specifically designed to measure RSC; it was designed to measure aberrant driving behaviours, primarily errors and violations. The comparison of road safety behavior between countries should ideally be broader in scope and more multifaceted, as aggressive driving only represents one limited aspect of the driving behavior in a country. This is, for instance, indicated by the studies comparing the significance of different DBQ items in different countries [21]. Additionally, the present study also indicates that aggressive driving is of less relevance in Norway compared to Greece.

The most important reason that we operationalized several of the main variables using a relatively small number of items is that the study in general includes a relatively high number of variables. This is due to the broad scope of the study, e.g., examining the influence of culture at different levels (e.g., national, sectorial, organizational, peers), examining the importance of other explanatory variables for the safety behaviours and accident involvement of professional drivers (e.g., working conditions, company and sector characteristics) and private drivers (e.g., vehicle type, demographic variables). We therefore limited the number of items measuring each of the main variables, to avoid a too high total number of questions in the questionnaire. When we chose questions to measure the main variables, we chose items that have been found to be important in previous research (e.g., [21]). Measuring road safety behavior, we focused on DBQ items that were significantly different in previous studies comparing northern European and southern European countries and that predicted crash involvement (e.g., [20,21]). It would clearly also have been interesting to include more DBQ items in the national comparison, also to further test our hypothesis that only some DBQ items vary according to nationality. Moreover, it would also have been interesting to develop all the DBQ items into a scale measuring DBQ items as descriptive norms and apply this in cross-national studies. However, this was unfortunately not feasible given the total number of variables in the present study. Thus, it indicates an issue that could be examined in future research.

4.9.2. Representativeness of the Samples

When concluding about the existence of different national RSCs based on the present study, it is important to remember that the national samples not are entirely representative. We compared the demographic characteristics of the private drivers with aggregated data for private car license holders in the two countries, and found that women are under-represented in the Norwegian sample and that the proportions of car drivers of 55 years and older are under-represented in both the national samples, but especially in Greece. The analyses indicated that both variables were significantly related to less aggressive violations. The results also indicated that the level of education was higher in the Norwegian sample of private drivers, but comparable objective data on this are lacking. Moreover, Rhodes is not necessarily representative of Greek drivers in general. Despite the fact that the samples of private drivers probably are not entirely representative, we nevertheless suggest that we can draw conclusions about the existence of different national road safety cultures for three main reasons. First, we can use professional drivers as a reference group, which we can assume is representative, because they generally have the same gender, relatively similar age, and probably also the same level of education. Comparing the professional drivers on the most important aspect of the national RSC that we measure, i.e., aggressive driving, we see that the difference between the Norwegian (4.7 points) and the Greek (5.8 points) professional drivers is approximately the same difference as between the Norwegian (4.3 points) and Greek (5.7 points) private drivers. Second, we obtain similar results when we focus only on comparable groups, controlling for place of living, gender, sex, age, and education. Table 14 shows average scores for men from Oslo and Athens, with high school or 3–4 years of university education, and who are between 27 and 55 years on the four behavior variables in the study and the two variables for national road safety culture.

Table 14. Mean scores for men from Oslo (N = 94) and Athens (N = 74), between 27 and 55 years, with high school or 3–4 years of university education on the four behavior variables in the study and the two variables for national road safety culture. *p*-values are indicated (n.s. = not significant).

Country	Aggressive Violations	Over Speeding	Driving under the Influence	Lacking Seat Belt Use	National RSC: Aggr./Violations	National RSC: Compliance/Politen.
Norway	4.7	5.3	1.05	1.1	12.2	7.3
Greece	5.3	5.1	1.22	2.4	14.8	7.1
p-value	0.03	n.s.	0.02	0.00	0.00	n.s.

It should be noted that this comparison is not the same as making an assessment of representativeness. The populations of drivers in different countries have different demographic compositions (gender, age), and in several cases this can be one of the explanations for different national RSCs. However, the comparisons in Table 14 indicate that the differences we have seen between the national sample of private drivers do not appear to be due to different demographic compositions in the samples, or biased national samples.

Third, when controlling for these variables in the regression analyses, we still see significant differences between the groups on aggressive violations, and significant contributions of national RSC on behaviours. Also, when concluding about differences between subgroups in our samples, it is also important to remember that many of these subgroups are small, and that conclusions about their significance should be interpreted with caution. Rhodes respondents is a small group in our sample, and the sampled drivers may not necessarily be representative.

4.9.3. Self-Reported Data

The study is based on self-reported data, which could be influenced by respondents' memory, truthfulness, and social or psychological biases that may influence reporting. As noted by Nævestad et al. [22], comparing cross-cultural samples is challenging, as different national samples may be influenced by different baselines, and as expectations may vary between national samples. The levels of experience with surveys and trust in anonymity may vary between national samples [36]. It is difficult to conclude about this.

4.9.4. False Consensus?

A potential critique that can be raised against identification of the descriptive norms mechanism is that it also may influence behaviour through the false consensus bias, which involves that people overestimate the prevalence of risky behaviour among others to justify their own behavior [52]. The main argument against this contention is that, in the present study, we also measure the contribution of peer group RSC as descriptive norms, and we find the contribution of national RSC and peer RSC to differ substantially. Moreover, the relationships with respondents' different types of behaviours and national RSC and peer RSC vary in strengths, depending on the behaviour in question, and not all relationships are statistically significant. Thus, contrary to the false consensus mechanism, which implies that perceptions about the behaviours of others reflect respondents' own behaviours, we found that respondents' perceptions of other drivers' behaviour differed according to the groups and behaviour in question.

4.9.5. Future Research Should Include More Countries

Norway and Greece are very different when it comes to road safety management and performance. Thus, it can be argued that it is difficult to conduct a systematic comparison of the countries, as they differ in many respects. Although the contrast between Norway and Greece has been instructive in the present study to highlight differences, it can for instance be argued that also including more countries that are more similar to those already included would enable us to test hypotheses more robustly.

4.9.6. Further Theoretical Development of the Relationship between National RSC and Behaviours

We operationalize national RSC as descriptive norms, inducing a mild social pressure to behave in certain ways. It should, however, be noted that social psychological research already has well-developed conceptualizations of the relationships between norms and behaviour. The theory of planned behaviour (TPB), for instance, identifies descriptive norms as just one of several predictors of behaviour (e.g., attitudes, perceived behavioural control, intentions) (cf. [62]). Future research should examine how our conceptualization of national RSC can be adapted to e.g., TPB. Another interesting approach is provided by Naveh and Katz Navon [63], distinguishing between compliance and internalization. These processes can also describe the relationship between national RSC and behaviour, including how RSC is (re)created. First, drivers may behave in line with norms if they know they will be sanctioned by other drivers if they do not. This is externally motivated influence from social norms on behavior: "compliance" [63]. Second, drivers' norm-compliant behaviour can be internally motivated, through "internalization", involving processes where drivers learn about norms and gradually recognize their importance and value until they accept them as their own [63]. Internalized norms are often linked to our identity, our assessments of morality, and our feelings. This was especially illustrated in the qualitative interviews with the Norwegian drivers, who for instance stated that they would only drive under the influence of alcohol "if someone's life depended on it".

4.9.7. The (Possible) Interaction between National Road Safety Culture and Personality

Several studies also focus on the relationships between personality traits and driver behaviour (e.g., [64,65]). Ju et al. [65], found that decision-making in an extreme, simulated accident situation is critically influenced by personality traits. Stephens et al. [64] explored the influence of anger and anxiety traits on driver evaluations and behaviour, and found that all drivers become angry when impeded, or in other anger-provoking situations, and that only drivers with high trait anger become angry and behaved aggressively in circumstances most would not consider provocative. These studies are very interesting, as they may direct attention to how personality traits may interact with the national RSC. Future studies could, e.g., compare drivers with high anger traits in national RSC with different levels of aggression (e.g., Norway versus Greece).

5. Conclusions

In this study, we have measured national RSC as descriptive norms, hypothesizing that the mechanisms between national RSC and road safety behaviour is drivers' perception of what is "normal" and expected from drivers within their country, generating a mild social pressure to behave in certain ways. Our study indicates that the main differences between the Norwegian and the Greek RSCs first relate to the higher prevalence of aggressive violations in Greece, which we have found to be related to accident involvement. Focusing especially on aggressive violations, we found more similarities between professional and private drivers within Norway and Greece than between the groups across countries. Greek drivers generally attributed higher levels of aggression and violations to other drivers in their country, while Norwegian drivers attributed higher levels of compliance and politeness to other drivers from their country. We suggested that the different RSCs may be due to differences in: (1) interaction, (2) infrastructure, (3) enforcement, (4) education, (5) road user composition, and (6) perhaps also the financial crisis. The specific importance of these factors and possible additional factors is an issue requiring further research. A key result of the present study is that RSC is not only created at the national level. We found that respondents' memberships in several different sociocultural groups influenced their safety behaviours, e.g., being a professional driver, organizations, peer groups, and geographically enclosed areas. The present study indicates that national road safety culture is important, as it influences road safety behaviours, which in turn are related to accident involvement. Based on this, we have suggested that the concept of national RSC may be evoked to shed light on the different national accident records of Norway and Greece. In accordance with Edwards et al. [5], our study indicates that the RSC within a given nation may be comprised by a series of nested cultures, at different levels and in different contexts. The main strength of the RSC perspective, which has been illustrated in the present study, is that it indicates the power of social ties for road safety, or more specifically the importance of sociocultural group memberships for road safety behaviours. Although it may be argued that a lack of consensus on definitions may raise profound concerns with the value and validity of the RSC concept, the concept still is relatively unstudied, and more research is needed to develop definitions, theories, and measurement tools. More research is also needed on how the RSC perspective can inform preventive measures.

Author Contributions: Conceptualization: T.O.N., A.L., R.O.P, T.B., G.Y., Methodology: T.O.N., R.O.P., A.L., G.Y., T.B., Validation: T.O., Formal Analysis: T.O.N., A.L., Writing-Original Draft Preparation, T.O.N., A.L, R.O.P., T.B., G.Y., Writing-Review & Editing: TON, Project Administration, TON: Funding Acquisition: T.O.N., T.B., R.O.P., A.L, G.Y.

Funding: This research was funded by the Norwegian Research Council's Transport 2025 program. Grant number: 250298.

Acknowledgments: In this section you can acknowledge any support given which is not covered by the author contribution or funding sections. This may include administrative and technical support, or donations in kind (e.g., materials used for experiments).

Conflicts of Interest: The authors declare no conflict of interest.

References

1. WHO. 2018. Available online: https://www.who.int/news-room/fact-sheets/detail/road-traffic-injuries (accessed on 1 February 2019).
2. Elvik, R.; Høye, A.; Vaa, T.; Sørensen, M. *The Handbook of Road Safety Measures*, 2nd ed.; Emerald Insight: Bingley, UK, 2009.

3. Ward, N.J.; Linkenbach, J.; Keller, S.N.; Otto, J. *White Paper on Traffic Safety Culture. 2010: White Papers for "Toward Zero Deaths: A National Strategy for Highway Safety" Series–White Paper No. 2*; Montana State University: Bozeman, MT, USA, 2010.
4. Nævestad, T.-O.; Bjørnskau, T. How Can the Safety Culture Perspective be Applied to Road Traffic? *Transp. Rev.* **2012**, *32*, 139–154. [CrossRef]
5. Edwards, J.; Freeman, J.; Soole, D.; Watson, B. A framework for conceptualising traffic safety culture. *Transp. Res. F: Psychol. Behav.* **2014**, *26*, 293–302. [CrossRef]
6. Christian, M.S.; Bradley, J.C.; Wallace, J.C.; Burke, M.J. Workplace safety: A meta-analysis of the role of person and situation factors. *J. Appl. Psychol.* **2009**, *94*, 1103–1127. [CrossRef]
7. Nahrgang, J.; Morgeson, F.; Hofmann, D. Safety at work: A meta-analytic investigation of the link between job demands, job resources, burnout, engagement, and safety outcomes. *J. Appl. Psychol.* **2011**, *96*, 71–94. [CrossRef]
8. Hudson, P. Applying the lessons of high risk industries to health care. *Qual. Saf. Heal. Care* **2003**, *12*, i7–i12. [CrossRef]
9. Reason, J. *Managing the Risk of Organisational Accidents*; Ashgate: Aldershot, UK, 1997.
10. Lappalainen, F.J.; Kuronen, J.; Tapaninen, U. Evaluation of the ISM Code in the Finnish shipping companies. *J. Marit. Res.* **2012**, *9*, 23–32.
11. Zuschlag, M.; Ranney, J.M.; Coplen, M. Evaluation of a safety culture intervention for Union Pacific shows improved safety and safety culture. *Saf. Sci.* **2016**, *83*, 59–73. [CrossRef]
12. Davey, J.; Freeman, J.; Wishart, D. A study predicting crashes among a sample of fleet drivers. In Proceedings of the Road Safety Research, Policing and Education Conference, Gold Coast, Australia, 25–27 October 2006.
13. Öz, B.; Ozkan, T.; Lajunen, T. An investigation of professional drivers: Organizational safety climate, driver behaviours and performance. *Transp. Res. Part F* **2013**, *16*, 81–91. [CrossRef]
14. Wills, A.R.; Biggs, H.C.; Watson, B. Analysis of a safety climate measure for occupational vehicle drivers and implications for safer workplaces. *Aust. J. Rehabil. Counsel.* **2005**, *11*, 8–21. [CrossRef]
15. Huang, Y.; Zohar, D.; Robertson, M.M.; Garabet, A.; Lee, J.; Murphy, L.A. Development and validation of safety climate scales for lone workers using truck drivers as exemplar. *Transp. Res. Part F* **2013**, *17*, 5–19. [CrossRef]
16. Nævestad, T.-O. Cultures, Crises and Campaigns: Examining the Role of Safety Culture in the Management of Hazards in a High Risk Industry. Ph.D. Dissertation, Centre for Technology, Innovation and Culture, Faculty of Social Sciences, University of Oslo, Oslo, Norway, 2010.
17. Flin, R.; Mearns, K.; O'Connor, P.; Bryden, R. Measuring safety climate: Identifying the common features. *Saf. Sci.* **2000**, *34*, 177–192. [CrossRef]
18. Nævestad, T.-O.; Phillips, R.O.; Elvebakk, B. Traffic accidents triggered by drivers at work—A survey and analysis of contributing factors. *Transp. Res. Part F Psychol. Behav.* **2015**, *34*, 94–107. [CrossRef]
19. Luria, G.; Boehm, A.; Mazor, T. Conceptualizing and measuring community road-safety climate. *Saf. Sci.* **2014**, *70*, 288–294. [CrossRef]
20. Özkan, T.; Lajunen, T.; Chliaoutakis, J.E.; Parker, D.; Summala, H. Cross-cultural differences in driving behaviours: A comparison of six countries. *Transp. Res. Part F* **2006**, *9*, 227–242. [CrossRef]
21. Warner, H.W.; Özkan, T.; Lajunen, T.; Tzamalouka, G. Cross-cultural comparison of drivers' tendency to commit different aberrant driving behaviours. *Transp. Res. Part F* **2011**, *14*, 390–399. [CrossRef]
22. Nævestad, T.-O.; Phililps, R.O.; Laiuou, A.; Bjørnskau, T.; Yannis, G. Safety culture in professional road transport in Norway and Greece. *Transp. Res. Part F* **2019**. under review.
23. European Transport Safety Council (ETSC). RANKING EU PROGRESS ON ROAD SAFETY, 12th Road Safety Performance Index Report. June 2018. Available online: https://etsc.eu/wp-content/uploads/PIN_AR_2018_final.pdf (accessed on 1 February 2019).
24. Yannis, G.; Papadimitrou, E. Road Safety in Greece. *Procedia-Soc. Behav. Sci.* **2012**, *48*, 2839–2848. [CrossRef]
25. OECD. 2015. Available online: http://www.oecd-ilibrary.org/sites/9789264183896-en/ (accessed on 1 February 2019).
26. DACOTA. 2011. Available online: http://ec.europa.eu/transport/road_safety/specialist/erso/pdf/country_overviews/dacota-country-overview-el_en.pdf (accessed on 15 January 2019).
27. Papadimitriou, E.; Yannis, G.; Muhlrad, N. Road safety management in Greece. In Proceedings of the 6th Pan-Hellenic Road Safety Conference, Athens, Greece, 12–13 March 2015.

28. Nævestad, T.-O.; Phililps, R.O.; Laiuou, A.; Yannis, G. Road safety culture among HGV drivers in Norway and Greece: Why do Greek HGV drivers commit more aggressive violations in traffic. In *Prevention of Accidents at Work, Proceedings of the 9th International Conference on the Prevention of Accidents at Work (WOS 2017), Prague, Czech Republic, 3–6 October 2017*; Bernatik, A., kocurkova, L., Jørgensen, K., Eds.; Taylor & Francis Group: Abingdon-on-Thames, UK, 2018.
29. Nævestad, T.-O.; Phillips, R.O.; Laiou, A.; Yannis, G. Safety culture in professional road transport in Norway and Greece. In Proceedings of the Road Safety & Simulation (RSS2017), Hague, The Netherlands, 17–19 October 2017.
30. Nævestad, T.-O.A.; Laiou, T.; Bjørnskau, R.O.; Phillips, G. Yannis Safety culture factors predicting safety outcomes among private and professional drivers in Norway and Greece. In Proceedings of the 7th Panhellenic Road Safety Conference (RSC), Larissa, Greece, 11–12 October 2018.
31. Nævestad, T.-O.; Phillips, R.O.; Bjørnskau, T.; Ranestad, K.; Laiou, A.; Yannis, G. *Trafikksikkerhetskultur i Norge og Hellas*; TØI-rapport: Oslo, Norway, 2019.
32. Reason, J.T.; Manstead, A.S.R.; Stradling, S.G.; Baxter, J.S.; Campbell, K. Errors and violations on the road: A real distinction? *Ergonomics* **1990**, *33*, 1315–1332. [CrossRef] [PubMed]
33. Lajunen, T.; Summala, H. Can we trust self-reports of driving? Effects of impression management on driver behaviour questionnaire responses. *Transp. Res. Part F* **2003**, *6*, 97–107. [CrossRef]
34. Parker, D.; Lajunen, T.; Stradling, S. Attitudinal predictors of aggressive driving violations. *Transp. Res. Part F* **1998**, *1*, 11–24. [CrossRef]
35. Sucha, M.; Sramkova, L.; Risser, R. The Manchester driver behaviour questionnaire: Self-reports of aberrant behaviour among Czech drivers. *Eur. Transp. Res. Rev.* **2014**. [CrossRef]
36. Nævestad, T.-O.; Phillips, R.; Levlin, G.M.; Hovi, I.B. Internationalization in Road Transport of Goods in Norway: Safety Outcomes, Risk Factors and Policy Implications. *Safety* **2017**, *3*, 22. [CrossRef]
37. Huang, S.; Ruscio, D.; Ariansyah, D.; Yi, J.; Bordegoni, M. Does the Familiarity of Road Regulation Contribute to Driving Violation? A Simulated Study on Familiar and Unfamiliar Road Intersections among Young Chinese Drivers. In *Advances in Human Aspects of Transportation*; Stanton, N., Ed.; Advances in Intelligent Systems and Computing; Springer: Cham, Switzerland, 2018; Volume 597.
38. European Transport Safety Council (ERSC). Drink Driving in Commercial Transport. 2010. Available online: https://etsc.eu/wp-content/uploads/Drink_Driving_in_Commercial_Transport.pdf (accessed on 15 January 2019).
39. NPRA «Norwegian Public Roads Administration». *Statens vegvesen. Tilstandsundersøkelse kap 1/2015-Bruk av Bilbelter*; Statens Vegvesen: Oslo, Norway, 2015.
40. Heavy Goods Vehicles and Buses-European Commission. Available online: https://ec.europa.eu/transport/road_safety/sites/roadsafety/files/pdf/statistics/dacota/bfs2016_hgvs.pdf (accessed on 1 February 2019).
41. Salminen, S. Traffic accidents during work and work commuting. *Int. J. Ind. Ergon.* **2000**, *26*, 75–85. [CrossRef]
42. Bjørnskau, T. *Risiko i veitrafikken 2013/14, TØI rapport 1448/2015*; Transportøkonomisk institutt: Oslo, Norway, 2015.
43. Özkan, T.; Lajunen, T. What causes the differences in driving between young men and women? The effects of gender roles and sex onyoung drivers' driving behaviour and self-assessment of skills. *Transp. Res. Part F* **2006**, *9*, 269–277. [CrossRef]
44. De Winter, J.C.; Dodou, D. The Driver Behaviour Questionnaire as a predictor of accidents: A meta-analysis. *J. Saf. Res.h* **2010**, *41*, 463–470. [CrossRef]
45. AAA. *Improving Traffic Safety Culture in The United States—The Journey Forward*; AAA: Washington, DC, USA, 2007.
46. Moeckli, J.; Lee, J.D. The making of driving cultures. In *Improving Traffic Safety Culture in the United States—The Journey Forward*; AAA: Washington, DC, USA, 2007; pp. 59–76.
47. Lonero, L. Finding the next cultural paradigm for road safety. In *Improving Traffic Safety Culture in the United States—The Journey Forward*; AAA: Washington, DC, USA, 2007; pp. 1–20.
48. Girasek, D.C. Towards operationalising and measuring the traffic safety culture construct. *Int. J. Injury Control Saf. Promot.* **2011**, *19*, 37–46. [CrossRef]
49. Rakauskas, M.E.; Ward, N.J.; Gerberich, G. Identification of differences between rural and urban safety cultures. *Accid. Anal. Prev.* **2009**, *41*, 931–937. [CrossRef]

50. Nævestad, T.-O.; Elvebakk, B.; Bjørnskau, T. Traffic safety culture among bicyclists– results from a Norwegian study. *Saf. Sci.* **2014**, *70*, 29–40. [CrossRef]
51. Tunnicliff, D.; Watson, B.; White, K.M.; Lewis, I.; Wishart, D. The social context of motorcycle riding and the key determinants influencing rider behaviour: A qualitative investigation. *Traffic Injury Prevent.* **2011**, *12*, 363–376. [CrossRef]
52. Cialdini, R.B.; Reno, R.R.; Kallgren, C.A. A focus theory of normative conduct: Recycling the concept of norms to reduce littering in public places. *J. Person. Soc. Psychol.* **1990**, *58*, 1015–1026. [CrossRef]
53. Berkowitz, A.D. An overview of the social norms approach. In *Changing the Culture of College Drinking: A Socially Situated Health Communication Campaign*; Lederman, L., Stewart, L., Eds.; Hampton Press: Creskill, NJ, USA, 2005; pp. 193–214.
54. GAIN (Global Aviation Network). *Operator's Flight Safety Handbook*. 2001. Available online: https://flightsafety.org/files/OFSH_english.pdf (accessed on 1 February 2019).
55. The Handbook of Road Safety Measures. 2019. Available online: https://tsh.toi.no/doc687.htm#anchor_22494-5orhttps://tsh.toi.no/doc684.htm#anchor_22457-30 (accessed on 15 January 2019).
56. Bjørnskau, T.; Sagberg, F. What do Novice Drivers Learn during the First Months of Driving? Improved Handling Skills or Improved Road User Interaction? In *Traffic and Transport Psychology Theory and Application*; Underwood, G., Ed.; Elsevier: Amsterdam, The Netherlands, 2005; pp. 129–140.
57. Bjørnskau, T.; Longva, F. *Sikkerhetskultur i Transport*; TØI rapport 1012/2009; Transportøkonomisk institutt: Oslo, Norway, 2009.
58. Koustanaï, A.; Boloix, E.; Van Elslande, P.; Bastien, C. Statistical analysis of "looked-but-failed-to-see" accidents: Highlighting the involvement of two distinct mechanisms. *Accid. Anal. Prevent.* **2008**, *40*, 461–469. [CrossRef]
59. Jackson, L.; Chapman, P.; Crundall, D. What happens next? Predicting other road users' behaviour as a function of driving experience and processing time. *Ergonomics* **2009**, *52*, 154–164. [CrossRef]
60. Bjørnskau, T. The Zebra crossing game—A game theoretic model to explain counter-rule interaction between cars and cyclists. In Proceedings of the Third International Cycling Safety Conference, Gothenburg, Sweden, 18–19 November 2014.
61. Linkenbach, J.; Perkins; Wesley, H. *Montana's MOST of Us Don't Drink and Drive Campaign: A Social Norms Strategy to Reduce Impaired Driving Among 21-to-34Year-Olds*; Report No. DOT HS 809 869; National Highway Traffic Safety Administration: Washington, DC, USA, 2005.
62. Ajzen, I. The theory of planned behaviour. *Org. Behav. Hum. Decis. Process.* **1991**, *50*, 179–211. [CrossRef]
63. Naveh, E.; Katz-Navon, T. A Longitudinal Study of an Intervention to Improve Road Safety Climate: Climate as an Organizational Boundary Spanner. *J. Appl. Psychol.* **2015**, *100*, 216–226. [CrossRef]
64. Stephens, A.; Groeger, J.A. Situational specificity of trait influences on drivers' appraisals and driving behavior. *Transp. Res. Part F Traffic Psychol. Behav.* **2009**, *12*, 29–39. [CrossRef]
65. Ju, U.; Kang, J.; Wallraven, C. To Brake or Not to Brake? Personality Traits Predict Decision-Making in an Accident Situation. *Front. Psychol.* **2019**, *10*, 134. [CrossRef]

© 2019 by the authors. Licensee MDPI, Basel, Switzerland. This article is an open access article distributed under the terms and conditions of the Creative Commons Attribution (CC BY) license (http://creativecommons.org/licenses/by/4.0/).

 safety

Article

Driving Behaviour in Depression: Findings from a Driving Simulator Study

Vagioula Tsoutsi [1,2,*], Dimitris Dikeos [1], Maria Basta [3] and Maria Papadakaki [2]

[1] Sleep Study Unit, Eginition Hospital, First Department of Psychiatry, Medical School, National and Kapodistrian University of Athens, 11528 Athens, Greece; ddikeos@med.uoa.gr
[2] Laboratory of Health and Road Safety, Department of Social Work, Hellenic Mediterranean University, Heraklion, 71004 Crete, Greece; mpapadakaki@yahoo.gr
[3] Department of Psychiatry, University Hospital of Heraklion, 71110 Crete, Greece; mbasta73@gmail.com
* Correspondence: vagia.ts@gmail.com; Tel.: +30-693-8147-615

Received: 4 September 2019; Accepted: 12 October 2019; Published: 16 October 2019

Abstract: Depression is characterized by mental, emotional and executive dysfunction. Among its symptoms, sleep disturbance and anxiety are very common. The effects of depression and its treatment may have an impact on driving behaviour. In order to evaluate driving performance in depression, 13 patients and 18 healthy controls completed questionnaires and scales and were tested in a driving simulator. Driving simulator data included lateral position (LP), speed and distance from the preceding vehicle. History of collisions was associated with depression, body mass index (BMI) and next-day consequences of sleep disturbance. Aggressive driving was associated with fatigue and sleep disturbances. Concerning driving simulator data, a reduced ability to maintain constant vehicle velocity was positively correlated to BMI and insomnia. An LP towards the middle of the road was associated with anxiety. On the other hand, an LP towards the shoulder was associated with depression and next-day consequences of sleep disturbance, while a positive correlation was found between distance from the preceding vehicle and use of drugs with potential hypnotic effects; both these findings show that patients suffering from depression seem to realize the effects of certain symptoms on their driving ability and thus drive in a more defensive way than controls.

Keywords: depression; sleep disorders; anxiety; drugs; driving; driving simulator

1. Introduction

Sleep and vigilance, important factors which may have an impact on driving behaviour, are often affected by mental disorders and the effects of their treatment. Sleep disorders, excessive daytime sleepiness and drowsiness are the most common factors that lead to road collisions [1–4]. According to epidemiological studies, almost 50% of the population will experience some kind of mental illness at least once in their life, while 25% have experienced a mental disorder over the past year [5].

Depression and road accidents are among the four leading causes of morbidity and mortality in developed countries [6]. Depression, a quite common disease in the general population, is characterized by mental, emotional and executive dysfunction [7]. Depression affects psychomotor and cognitive skills [8], while its symptoms or adverse reactions to antidepressant treatment, which often include lethargy and other sleep disorders, may also affect functional level and have an impact on driving behaviour [7,9].

Driving is an almost daily activity for a large part of the world's population. It is a very complex process due to the limited time that the driver has in order to make a decision and react properly. There are specific abilities that are essential for driving; among them, visual perception, selective attention, vigilance, reactivity and stress tolerance are the most important [10].

The majority of studies on road accidents have focused on socio-demographic characteristics and general personality, as well as driving competence [11,12]. While a small number of research studies have examined driving performance in relation to depression and anxiety, their main focus is often on the effects of the drugs, especially antidepressants and benzodiazepines [7,10,13,14].

The driving simulator is a device which reliably reflects driving performance on the road and has been used in studies under a variety of conditions potentially affecting driving ability (e.g., alcohol consumption and blood levels, sleep deprivation, sleep apnea, use of mobile phone, etc.) [15–17].

The aim of the current study is to evaluate driving performance in depression on a driving simulator, taking into account levels of anxiety and sleep disturbance.

2. Methods

2.1. Participants and Design

The current study is a comparison of driving performance in depressed patients and a group of healthy controls. A sample of 13 depressed patients (all but one receiving antidepressant treatment) and 18 healthy controls participated in this study. The patients who participated were diagnosed and monitored by a psychiatrist.

Participants were included if they met the following criteria: Age 18 years or older, possession of a driving license, driving regularly and informed consent prior to participation. The study had two parts. In the first part, participants were interviewed by the researcher and were asked to complete questionnaires and scales; in the second part they were evaluated for their driving on a VS500M driving simulator (Virage Simulation, Canada).

2.2. Questionnaires

The choice of questionnaires/scales was based on findings of previous literature which have shown that sleep disturbance [1–4,9], day-time somnolence [1–4], low functioning [10] and driving behaviour [11–13] are very often factors underlying road traffic collisions, and on the fact that the scales we used in the study have been extensively utilized in studies of depressed patients as well as in studies of driving performance.

2.2.1. Demographics and Other Data

A questionnaire was used to document information about age, sex, marital status, educational level, profession, years since acquiring driver's license and history of collisions (irrespective of responsibility) involved as a driver.

2.2.2. Medical History

Information about history of mental and somatic disorders, current medications and current mental state were recorded.

2.2.3. Hospital Anxiety and Depression Scale (HADS)

The hospital anxiety and depression scale was designed by Zigmond and Snaith [18]. It is a self-reported scale that consists of 14 items and each of these items has four possible answers (0–3). It is designed in order to estimate separately anxiety (HADS-A) and depression (HADS-D).

2.2.4. Athens Insomnia Scale (AIS)

The Athens insomnia scale is a self-reported questionnaire [19] estimating the difficulty in sleep according to ICD-10 criteria [20]. It consists of eight four-point Lickert scale (0–3) items, the first five of them pertaining to sleep induction, nighttime awakenings, final awakening, total sleep duration and quality of sleep, while the last three cover next-day wellbeing, functioning capacity and sleepiness during the day.

2.2.5. Fatigue Severity Scale (FSS)

The fatigue severity scale was designed in 1989 [21]. It is a self-reported questionnaire consisting of nine items which estimate the severity of the symptoms of fatigue. The score of each item ranges from 1 to 7, where 1 is "strongly disagree" and 7 is "strongly agree".

2.2.6. Sleep Disturbances Questionnaire

This questionnaire was designed by the Sleep Study Unit of Eginition University Hospital. It is a self-reported questionnaire consisting of six items regarding the quality and disturbances of sleep (overall sleep satisfaction, movements, snoring, breathing, difficulty in sleep, drowsiness during the day, nightmares). The score of each item ranges from 0 to 3, where 0 is "never" and 3 is "always".

2.2.7. Social and Occupational Functioning Assessment Scale (SOFAS)

This scale reflects the estimation of the overall level of functioning by a clinician [22]. The rating ranges from 0 (lowest functioning) to 100. Both social and occupational functioning are considered, as well as any impairments due to physical or mental disorders. In order to be considered, the impairment should be the effect of a health problem and not just a consequence of a lack of opportunity or of an environment.

2.2.8. Driver Stress Inventory (DSI)

The driver stress inventory (DSI) aims to detect drivers' vulnerability to stress reactions while driving. It is an extension of the driving behaviour inventory (DBI) [23]. In this study we use the version of Qu et al. [24].

It is a self-reported questionnaire consisting of 48 items which estimates in five separate subscales aggression, dislike of driving, hazard monitoring, thrill seeking and proneness to fatigue. The score of each item ranges from 0 to 10, where 0 is "not at all" and 10 is "very much".

2.3. Driving Simulator

Driving Simulator «Virage VS500M» (Virage Simulation, Canada) features advanced simulation software and uses a sophisticated driving environment with real auto parts to provide a realistic feel in all functions. Driving Simulator's environment appears in Figure 1.

Figure 1. The driving simulator's environment.

It consists of an open cabin including the driver's seat, the center console, a fully functional instrument cluster, lights and warning lights as well as motion and vibration systems. Three-dimensional graphics are projected into three wide screens covering a 180 degree field of view and located in front of the cabin. The mirrors are inserted in the main screen. The driving simulator has a variety of different scenarios where the user can drive in many different environments, such as in the city, on the motorway and on the mountains, in different weather conditions, etc.

The Virage Series Simulators have been validated for transfer of training in control skills to real life with satisfactory results, although caution should be taken, since the only relevant study of the Virage Series refers to a truck simulator and not the car simulator which was used in the present study [25].

In this study we used three of the available scenarios. In scenario 1 participants drove without interference in a motorway environment for 5 min. In scenario 2 participants drove also for 5 min in a motorway environment but in this scenario an event (sudden obstacle in the road) was designed in order to record the participants' reaction. Participants were not informed beforehand about the event. Scenario 3 was a 5-minute drive in an urban environment. A 3-minute accustomization driving period preceded the three scenarios.

2.4. Statistical Analysis

The SPSS 23.0 statistical package (IBM SPSS Statistics for Windows, Version 23.0. Armonk, NY, USA: IBM Corp., 2015) was used to process the data. Multiple linear backward regressions were performed for each dependent variable and the final regression model was retained. For the backward regressions all subjects were pooled together; to make between-group comparisons clear, however, the means (± SD) of the group of depressed patients and of that of the controls were calculated and are presented in a separate table.

The independent variables were: Gender, age, marital status, variable patient/control, body mass index (BMI), years of possession of a driving license, drugs with potential hypnotic effects, score of HADS depression and HADS anxiety separately, total score of Athens insomnia scale (AIS), sum score of items 7 and 8 of Athens insomnia scale (next-day consequences of sleep disturbance), total score of fatigue severity scale (FSS), total score of sleep disturbances questionnaire and total score of SOFAS functioning scale.

The dependent variables were: History of self-reported involvement in road accidents, scores of the five subscales of the questionnaire for stress assessment during driving (DSI) and data extracted from the Driving Simulator, namely lateral position (LP), inability to keep a steady lateral position (expressed as standard deviation of lateral position as a metric of each participant), vehicle velocity (both as mean car speed of each participant, as well as inability to keep a steady speed expressed as standard deviation of car speed as a metric of each participant) and distance from the preceding vehicle. The lateral position is the distance of the middle of the vehicle from the middle of the lane in which the vehicle is driven. It varies from −1 to 1 with −1 signifying the car being at the limit of the lane towards the middle of the road (to the left in roads where traffic keeps to the right) and 1 signifying the car being at the limit of the lane towards the shoulder (to the right in roads where traffic keeps to the right). The width of the simulator's lane is 350 cm. In scenarios with multiple lanes −1 signifies a position towards the faster lane and 1 a position towards the slower lane.

Statistical significance level was set at 5%.

3. Results

3.1. Main Characteristics of the Sample

Table 1 displays the main characteristics of the 31 participants who were included in the study. The majority of participants were women, about half of the total sample were married or cohabited and the mean age was 46 years old (range 29 to 69). Twenty-seven participants were employed, all but one at a daytime job. Moreover, 27 had a higher education degree and 24 lived in an urban area. Mean time from acquiring a driver's license was 22.77 years (range 6 to 49).

3.2. Physical and Mental Characteristics of the Sample

The mean body mass index (BMI) was 25.06 (range 20 to 52, Table 1). Eighteen participants had no symptoms of depression and they had never received antidepressants, 12 participants were diagnosed with depression and they were under antidepressant treatment and one had depression but was not receiving antidepressant treatment.

Table 1. Main characteristics of the sample.

	Participant Profile		
	N (%)		
	Total (N = 31)	Depressed (N = 13)	Controls (N = 18)
Female	23 (74.2)	10 (76.9)	13 (72.2)
Married or cohabiting	14 (45.2)	6 (46.2)	8 (44.4)
Employed	27 (87.1)	9 (69.2)	18 (100)
High education	27 (87.1)	10 (76.9)	17 (94.4)
Urban residents	24 (77.4)	9 (69.2)	15 (83.3)
Age	46.00 ± 10.23 *	47.77 ± 10.57 *	44.72 ± 10.09 *
BMI	25.06 ± 5.63 *	25.75 ± 8.30 *	24.57 ± 2.59 *
Years of possessing a driving license	22.77 ± 6.37 *	21.92 ± 5.31 *	23.39 ± 7.12 *

* Mean, Standard Deviation.

3.3. Main Findings from the Final Models of Multiple Backward Regressions

The mean values of patients with depression and healthy controls regarding the five variables for which significant results were found in the regressions are presented in Table 2.

Table 2. Frequencies (%) or mean values (± standard deviation) of the groups of patients and controls.

Variables	Depressed	Controls
History of collisions	4 out of 13 (30.8%)	4 out of 18 (22.3%)
Aggressive driving score [1]	4.43 ± 0.79	4.45 ± 1.01
Speed SD [2]	5.48 ± 1.24	5.09 ± 1.42
Mean LP [3]	0.26 ± 0.82	0.53 ± 0.89
Mean of distance from the preceding vehicle (in meters)	29.57 ± 60.41	16.71 ± 21.83

[1]: Subcale on aggressive driving of the driving stress inventory; [2]: Standard deviation of speed (inability to keep constant vehicle velocity) in the driving simulator; [3]: Mean of lateral position; negative numbers: Towards the middle of the road (faster lane); positive numbers: Towards the shoulder (slower lane) in the driving simulator.

The main findings from the final models of multiple backward regressions are presented in Table 3. History of collisions and a high risk score on the DSI subscale for "aggressive driving" were the two variables derived by questionnaires for which significant associations were found with some of the independent variables. From the variables derived from the driving simulator output, those which showed significant associations to independent variables were the ability to maintain a constant vehicle velocity (expressed by the standard deviation of speed), lateral position and the distance from the preceding vehicle.

As shown in Table 3, history of collisions was positively correlated with BMI, with subjects with no collisions in their history having a mean BMI of 24.12 (standard deviation: 2.86) and those with one or more past collisions a mean BMI of 27.79 (SD: 9.94). HADS-D score and sum score of items 7 and 8 of the AIS (next-day consequences of sleep disturbance) were also correlated with number of past collisions. Aggressive driving was positively correlated with the total score on the fatigue severity scale and with total score on sleep disturbances questionnaire and it was negatively correlated to HADS-D score, the sum score of items 7 and 8 of the AIS (next-day consequences of sleep disturbance) and SOFAS (overall functioning) scale. The standard deviation of speed (i.e., the inability to maintain constant velocity) was positively correlated to BMI and AIS total score. Driving towards the middle of the road (faster lane) was positively correlated to the HADS-A score and driving towards the shoulder of the road (slower lane) was positively correlated to the HADS-D score and the sum score of items 7 and 8 of the AIS. The distance from the preceding vehicle was positively correlated to being on drugs with potential hypnotic effects. Those patients who received drugs with potential hypnotic effects kept a mean distance from the preceding vehicle of 73.52m (SD: 103.33) while the mean distance of all other participants was 14.49m (SD: 18.57).

Table 3. Main findings from the final models of multiple backward regressions.

Dependent Variables	Independent Variables								
	BMI [1]	HADSD [2]	HADSA [3]	AIS [4]	AIS7-8 [5]	FSS [6]	SOFAS [7]	SD [8]	DRUGS [9]
History of Collisions	β = 0.073 p = 0.003	β = 0.104 p = 0.001			β = 0.279 p = 0.002				
Aggressive Driving [a]		β = −0.101 p = 0.028			β = −0.372 p = 0.009	β = 0.040 p = 0.002	β = −0.067 p = 0.012	β = 0.157 p = 0.035	
Speed SD [b]	β = 0.110 p = 0.013			β = 0.183 p = 0.021					
Mean LP [c]		β = 0.121 p = 0.026	β = −0.128 p = 0.017		β = 0.298 p = 0.041				
Mean distance [d]									β = 590.27 p = 0.007

β = multiple regression coefficient; p = statistical significance. [a]: Subscale on aggressive driving of the driving stress inventory; [b]: Standard deviation of speed (inability to keep constant vehicle velocity) in the driving simulator; [c]: Mean of lateral position; negative numbers: Towards the middle of the road (faster lane); positive numbers: Towards the shoulder (slower lane) in the driving simulator; [d]: Mean of the distance from the preceding vehicle. [1]: Body mass index; [2]: Hospital anxiety and depression scale depression score; [3]: Hospital anxiety and depression scale anxiety score; [4]: Athens insomnia scale (total score); [5]: Low functioning and somnolence (sum score of items 7 and 8 of the AIS); [6]: Fatigue severity scale; [7]: Social and occupational functioning assessment scale; [8]: Sleep disturbances questionnaire; [9]: Drugs with potential hypnotic effects.

4. Discussion

Based on our results, it was shown that depression, as it was assessed by HADS-D on the day of the experiment, was positively correlated to a history of road collisions (p = 0.001). The number of past collisions was also positively correlated with body mass index (p = 0.003) and the next-day consequences of sleep disturbance (low functioning and somnolence, sum score of items 7 and 8 of the AIS) (p = 0.002). Similar to our findings relating to depression, a study has found that, independent of the intensity of depression (mild, moderate, severe), the probability for depressive patients causing collisions is 2.4 times than that of the non-depressed [13]. Regarding somnolence and low daytime functioning due to sleep disturbance, our findings are in accordance with studies [1,26] which have provided evidence that daytime somnolence is strongly positively correlated with collisions. High BMI has also been found to be a risk factor for collisions [2], also in patients with obstructive sleep apnea [27].

Aggression during driving (as assessed by DSI) was negatively correlated to depression; responses of the control group showed higher aggressive driving than those of depressed patients. On the other hand, driving aggression showed a strong positive correlation with the variables fatigue and sleep disturbances (p = 0.002 and p = 0.035, respectively). The more the participants reported fatigue and disturbed sleep, the more aggression during driving was found through the questionnaires that assessed driving behaviour. Research on collisions that were caused due to sleep disturbances has shown that, similar to our findings, daytime sleepiness was found to be the most important risk factor [1,2,28]. These findings imply that poor sleep quality may lead to mismanagement of emotions and that may eventually contribute to collisions. In a meta-analysis study of Zhang et al. [29] aggressive driving was strongly correlated to driving anger, which can lead to frustration and cognitive difficulties (attention, reasoning, judgment and decision making) during driving.

The reduced ability to maintain constant vehicle velocity was positively correlated to body mass index and to the total score in the AIS (p = 0.013 and p = 0.021, respectively). Garbarino et al. [4] found also that insomnia is positively correlated to road accidents. Our findings show that insomnia affects the ability to maintain constant vehicle velocity, which might lead to collisions since the driver is not adequately controlling the vehicle's speed. Regarding BMI, research shows that it is a risk factor for traffic accidents [2,30]. The main connection of BMI to road safety is that a high BMI is strongly associated with the risk for obstructive sleep apnea and the presence of excessive daytime sleepiness [31].

Anxiety was found to be associated with a trend to drive towards the middle of the road (LP-faster lane) (p = 0.017). To the contrary, a tendency to drive towards the shoulder of the road (LP-slower lane) was associated with the intensity of depression (p = 0.026) and next-day consequences of sleep disturbance (low functioning and somnolence, sum score of items 7 and 8 on AIS) (p = 0.041) denoting that drivers were driving more cautiously.

Similarly, a strong positive correlation was found between the distance from the preceding vehicle and being on drugs with potential hypnotic effects (p = 0.007). It seems that participants who were under this kind of medication were keeping a larger safety distance from the preceding vehicle. The fact that depression, consequences of sleep disturbances and use of drugs with possible hypnotic activity lead to a more a "conservative" way of driving could be the result of an effort on the part of the patients to balance the dangers created by the consequences of depression and sleepiness while driving. This is a possible explanation why, in the study of Brunnauer et al. [10], which took place in a real driving environment (on-road driving test) and not in a driving simulator, no difference in driving skills was found between groups under medication and healthy controls.

The above findings, if supported by future studies, suggest that the main reason for any driving impairment of depressed patients is depression per se, its symptoms and its severity. The consequences of treatment, even with drugs which are considered to cause somnolence, do not seem to compromise safety. It should be, thus, understood that it is more important for road safety that patients with depression receive adequate therapeutic interventions for their condition, in spite of fears that the treatment might compromise their driving. This suggestion, however, is quite preliminary, given the small sample on which this study is based. Finally, clinical judgment should always be used in the decision whether to suggest to the patient that they avoid driving.

5. Limitations

Our sample being relatively small did not allow for a more detailed analysis to deal with confounding issues. Thus, the question if it is the comorbidities of depression (obesity, lack of sleep, etc.) that are associated with driving impairment or depression itself could not be addressed.

The generalization of the findings of the present study may be limited, since no information was available on how much the participants drive daily/weekly/monthly. Thus, it is difficult to know how far our sample is representative of the population at large or depressive patients for whom, in addition, there are no reliable data on their driving habits.

6. Conclusions

In this study, we examined driving performance in depression, taking into account the symptoms of anxiety and sleep disorders. The study was based on questionnaires and on driving in a driving simulator. The findings show that depression, sleep and anxiety measures correlated with various aspects of driving behaviour. Patients may have been using compensatory mechanisms to counteract some of the effects of depression and its treatment on their driving performance. These findings should be replicated in further studies in which questions of comorbidities, confounding factors and generalization of results need also to be addressed. Such a progress in our understanding of the field could lead to the development of road safety policy recommendations regarding depression and its treatment.

Author Contributions: Conceptualization, V.T., D.D. and M.P.; Data curation, V.T. and D.D.; Formal analysis, V.T. and D.D.; Investigation, V.T.; Methodology, V.T. and D.D.; Project administration, V.T.; Resources, M.B. and M.P.; Supervision, D.D.; Validation, V.T., D.D., M.B. and M.P.; Visualization, V.T.; Writing—original draft, V.T.; Writing—review and editing, D.D. and M.P.

Funding: This research received no external funding. The study has been conducted in the frame of an MSc Degree "Promotion of Mental Health-Prevention of Psychiatric Disorders", Medical School, National and Kapodistrian University of Athens.

Acknowledgments: Many thanks to the psychiatrists Th. Adrakta and E. Grinakis who recruited four patients for the study.

Conflicts of Interest: The authors declare no conflict of interest regarding this work.

Research Ethics: All participants gave their informed consent for inclusion before they participated in this study. The study was conducted in accordance with the Declaration of Helsinki and the protocol was approved by the Ethics Committee of University General Hospital of Heraklion (798/20/25-7-2018).

References

1. Inoue, Y.; Komada, Y. Sleep loss, sleep disorders and driving accidents. *Sleep Biol. Rythms* **2014**, *12*, 96–105. [CrossRef]
2. Johnson, K.D.; Patel, S.R.; Baur, D.M.; Edens, E.; Sherry, P.; Malhotra, A.; Kales, S.N. Association of sleep habits with accidents and near misses in United States transportation operators. *J. Occup. Environ. Med.* **2014**, *56*, 510–515. [CrossRef] [PubMed]
3. Barger, L.K.; Rajaratham, S.M.; Wang, W.; O'Brien, C.S.; Sullivan, J.P.; Qadri, S.; Lockley, S.W.; Czeisler, C.A. Common sleep disorders increase risk of motor vehicle crashes and Adverse Health Outcomes in Firefighters. *J. Clin. Sleep Med.* **2015**, *11*, 233–240. [CrossRef] [PubMed]
4. Garbarino, S.; Magravita, N.; Guglielmi, O.; Maestri, M.; Dini, G.; Bersi, F.M.; Toletone, A.; Chiorri, C.; Durando, P. Insomnia is associated with road accidents. Further evidence from a study on truck drivers. *PLoS ONE* **2017**, *12*, e0187256. [CrossRef] [PubMed]
5. Wittchen, H.-U.; Mühlig, S.; Beesdo, K. Mental disorders in primary care. *Dialogues Clin. Neurosci.* **2003**, *5*, 115–128.

6. WHO. *The Global Burden of Disease: 2004 Update*; World Health Organization: Geneva, Switzerland, 2008; pp. 1–160.
7. Van der Sluiszen, N.N.; Wingen, M.; Vermeeren, A.; Vinckenbosch, F.; Jongen, S.; Ramaekers, J.G. Driving performance of depressed patients who are untreated or receive long-term antidepressant (SSRI/SNRI) treatment. *Pharmacopsychiatry* **2017**, *50*, 182–188. [CrossRef]
8. Marazziti, D.; Consoli, G. Cognitive impairment in major depression. *Eur. J. Pharmacol.* **2010**, *626*, 83–86. [CrossRef]
9. Ferentinos, P.; Kontaxakis, V.; Havaki-Kontaxaki, B.; Paparrigopoulos, T.; Dikeos, D.; Ktonas, P.; Soldatos, C. Sleep disturbances in relation to fatigue in major depression. *J. Psychosom. Res.* **2009**, *66*, 37–42. [CrossRef]
10. Brunnauer, A.; Buschert, V.; Fric, M.; Distler, G.; Sander, K.; Segmiller, F.; Zwanzger, P.; Laux, G. Driving performance and psychomotor function in depressed patients treated with Agomelatine or Venlafaxine. *Pharmacopsychiatry* **2015**, *48*, 65–71. [CrossRef]
11. Chliaoutakis, J.E.; Demakakos, P.; Tzamalouka, G.; Bakou, V.; Koumaki, M.; Darviri, C. Aggressive behaviour while driving as predictor of self-reported road crashes. *J. Saf. Res.* **2002**, *33*, 431–443. [CrossRef]
12. Taubman-Ben-Ari, O.; Mikulincer, M.; Gillath, O. The multidimensional driving style inventory—Scale construct and validation. *Accid. Anal. Prev.* **2004**, *36*, 323–332. [CrossRef]
13. Alavi, S.S.; Mohammadi, M.R.; Souri, H.; Kalhori, S.M.; Jannatifard, F.; Sepahbodi, G. Personality, driving behaviour and mental disorders factors as predictors of road traffic accidents based on logistic regression. *Iran J. Med. Sci.* **2017**, *42*, 24–31. [PubMed]
14. Van der Sluiszen, N.N.; Vermeeren, A.; Jongen, S.; Vinckenbosch, F.; Ramaekers, J.G. Influence of Long-Term Benzodiazepine use on Neurogognitive Skills Related on Driving Performance in Patients Populations: A Review. *Pharmacopsychiatry* **2017**, *50*, 189–196. [CrossRef] [PubMed]
15. Blana, E. *Driving Simulator Validation Studies: A Literature Review*; Working Paper; University of Leeds: Leeds, UK, 1996.
16. Helland, A.; Jenssen, G.D.; Lervåg, L.E.; Westin, A.A.; Moen, T.; Sakshaug, K.; Lydersen, S.; Mørland, J.; Slørdal, L. Comparison of driving simulator performance with real driving after alcohol intake: A randomized, single blind, placebo-controlled, cross-over trial. *Accid. Anal. Prev.* **2013**, *53*, 9–16. [CrossRef] [PubMed]
17. Papadakaki, M.; Tzamalouka, G.; Gnardellis, C.; Lajunen, T.J.; Chliaoutakis, J. Driving performance while using a mobile phone: A simulation study of Greek professional drivers. *Transp. Res. (Part F)* **2016**, *38*, 164–170. [CrossRef]
18. Zigmond, S.A.; Snaith, R.P. The hospital anxiety and depression scale. *Acta Psychiatr. Scand.* **1983**, *67*, 361–370. [CrossRef]
19. Soldatos, C.R.; Dikeos, D.G.; Paparrigopoulos, T. Athens Insomnia Scale: Validation of an instrument based on ICD-10 criteria. *J. Psychosom. Res.* **2000**, *48*, 555–560. [CrossRef]
20. WHO. *The ICD-10 Classification of Mental and Behavioural Disorders: Clinical Descriptions and Diagnostic Guidelines*; World Health Organization: Geneva, Switzerland, 1992.
21. Krupp, L.B.; LaRocca, N.G.; Muir-Nash, J.; Steinberg, A.D. The fatigue severity scale. Application to patients with multiple Sclerosis and Systemic Lupus Erythematosus. *Arch. Neurol.* **1989**, *46*, 1121–1123. [CrossRef]
22. Goldman, H.; Skodol, A.; Lave, T. Revising Axis V for DSM-IV: A Review of Measures of Social Functioning. *Am. J. Psychiatry* **1992**, *149*, 1148–1156. [CrossRef]
23. Glendon, A.I.; Dorn, L.; Matthews, G.; Gulian, E.; Davies, D.R.; Debney, L.M. Reliability of the driving behaviour inventory. *Ergonomics* **1993**, *36*, 719–726. [CrossRef]
24. Qu, W.; Zhang, Q.; Zhao, W.; Zhang, K.; Ge, Y. Validation of the Driver Stress Inventory in China: Relationship with dangerous driving behaviours. *Accid. Anal. Prev.* **2016**, *87*, 50–58. [CrossRef] [PubMed]
25. Hirsch, P.; Choukou, M.-A.; Bellavance, F. Transfer of training in basic control skills from truck simulator to real truck. *Transp. Res. Rec.* **2017**, *2637*, 67–73. [CrossRef]
26. Karimi, M.; Hedner, J.; Lombardi, C.; McNicholas, W.T.; Penzel, T.; Riha, R.L.; Rodenstein, D.; Grote, L.; Esada Study Group; Barbé, F.; et al. Driving habits and risk factors for traffic accidents among sleep apnea patients- a European multi-centre cohort study. *J. Sleep Res.* **2014**, *23*, 689–699. [CrossRef] [PubMed]
27. Nena, E.; Steiropoulos, P.; Tsara, V. Obstructive sleep apnea as a risk factor for road traffic accidents. *Arch. Hell. Med.* **2010**, *27*, 128–130. (In Greek)
28. Al Lawati, N.; Patel, S.; Ayas, N. Epidemiology, Risk factors and consequences of obstructive sleep apnea and short sleep duration. *Prog. Cardiovasc. Dis.* **2009**, *51*, 285–293. [CrossRef]

29. Zhang, T.; Chan, A. The association between driving anger and driving outcomes: A meta-analysis of evidence from the past twenty years. *Accid. Anal. Prev.* **2016**, *90*, 50–62. [CrossRef]
30. Philip, P.; Chaufton, C.; Orriols, L.; Lagarde, E.; Amoros, E.; Laumon, B.; Akerstedt, T.; Taillard, J.; Sagaspe, P. Complaints of poor sleep and risk of traffic accidents: A population-based case-control study. *PLoS ONE* **2014**, *9*, e114102. [CrossRef]
31. Kales, S.N.; Straubel, M.G. Obstructive sleep apnea in North American commercial drivers. *Ind. Health* **2014**, *52*, 13–24. [CrossRef]

© 2019 by the authors. Licensee MDPI, Basel, Switzerland. This article is an open access article distributed under the terms and conditions of the Creative Commons Attribution (CC BY) license (http://creativecommons.org/licenses/by/4.0/).

MDPI
St. Alban-Anlage 66
4052 Basel
Switzerland
Tel. +41 61 683 77 34
Fax +41 61 302 89 18
www.mdpi.com

Safety Editorial Office
E-mail: safety@mdpi.com
www.mdpi.com/journal/safety

www.ingramcontent.com/pod-product-compliance
Lightning Source LLC
LaVergne TN
LVHW071959080526
838202LV00064B/6792